Retro Recipes: A 1950s Culinary Journey
The Classic Cookbook of Post-War America

Olivia Wylde

Table of Contents:

Introduction

Step back in time with us to the vibrant 1950s, an era characterized by profound optimism, newfound prosperity, and culinary evolution. The decade's food scene danced to the rhythm of contrasting beats. As the United States embraced an era of abundance after the war, the American table was laden with diverse flavors, textures, and innovations. This cookbook offers a delightful culinary journey, exploring the emblematic recipes that graced the tables of the 1950s American households.

The 1950s heralded the ascent of convenient processed foods, revolutionizing the culinary landscape. Frozen dinners, canned foods, and instant mixes found a steadfast place in the kitchens, embodying the era's zeal for innovation and convenience. Despite the burgeoning allure of modern, time-saving options, traditional and homely recipes held a cherished spot in the American heart and hearth. This cookbook is a tribute to this dual culinary narrative, celebrating both the classic and the novel.

Each recipe in this collection has been meticulously curated to provide you with an authentic 1950s culinary experience. From the comforting embrace of homemade meatloaf to the avant-garde allure of molded gelatin salads, these dishes echo the culinary trends and traditions of the era, allowing you to relish the diverse tastes of the 1950s. Beyond mere recipes, this book is steeped in rich stories, offering a glimpse into the socio-cultural milieu of the decade. It aims to narrate the tale of a generation through its gastronomic preferences, creating a comprehensive and flavorful historical portrait.

Embark on this nostalgic culinary expedition and rediscover the tastes that defined a decade. May this cookbook be your time machine, transporting your senses to the lively and flavorful world of the 1950s. Enjoy the journey and bon appétit!

Breakfast

Classic Cheese and Tomato Sandwich

Ingredients:

- Sliced white bread (2 pieces)
- Sliced cheddar cheese (1 slice)
- Tomato slices
- Butter
- Salt and pepper to taste

Preparation:

1. Butter one side of each slice of bread.
2. Place the cheddar cheese and tomato slices on the unbuttered side of one bread slice.
3. Season with salt and pepper to taste.
4. Top with the second slice of bread, buttered side out.
5. Grill on a hot griddle or pan until the bread is toasted and the cheese is melted.
6. Cut diagonally and serve warm.

Nutritional Values: Calories: ~300 kcal, Protein: ~12g, Fat: ~18g, Carbohydrates: ~20g

1950s Trivia: In the 1950s, sandwiches were a popular choice for a quick and easy meal. The use of white bread and processed cheese reflects the era's shift towards convenient, processed foods.

Deviled Eggs

Ingredients:

- Eggs (6, hard-boiled)
- Mayonnaise (1/4 cup)
- Dijon mustard (1 teaspoon)
- Paprika (1/2 teaspoon, and extra for garnish)
- Salt and pepper to taste
- Chopped fresh parsley or chives for garnish

Preparation:

1. Cut the hard-boiled eggs in half lengthwise and remove the yolks.
2. Mash the yolks in a bowl and mix with mayonnaise, Dijon mustard, paprika, salt, and pepper.
3. Spoon or pipe the yolk mixture back into the egg whites.
4. Garnish with a sprinkle of paprika and chopped fresh parsley or chives.
5. Chill in the refrigerator before serving.

Nutritional Values: Calories: ~70 kcal per half egg, Protein: ~3g, Fat: ~5g, Carbohydrates: ~1g

1950s Trivia: Deviled eggs were a classic dish for parties and gatherings in the 1950s. Their simplicity, paired with a rich and creamy taste, made them a hit as an appetizer and snack.

Pineapple Upside Down Cake

Ingredients:

- Canned pineapple rings (7)
- Maraschino cherries (7)
- Brown sugar (1/2 cup)
- Unsalted butter (1/4 cup, melted)
- All-purpose flour (1 1/2 cups)
- Baking powder (2 tsp)
- Salt (1/2 tsp)
- Granulated sugar (1/2 cup)
- Egg (1)
- Milk (1 cup)
- Vanilla extract (1 tsp)

Preparation:

1. Preheat the oven to 350°F (175°C).
2. In a baking pan, spread melted butter evenly and sprinkle brown sugar over it.
3. Arrange the pineapple rings and place a maraschino cherry in the center of each ring.
4. In a bowl, sift together the flour, baking powder, and salt.
5. In another bowl, beat the egg and gradually add granulated sugar, beating until thick. Stir in vanilla extract.
6. Add the dry ingredients to the wet mixture alternatively with milk, mixing well each time.
7. Pour the batter over the pineapple rings in the baking pan.
8. Bake for 30-35 minutes or until a toothpick inserted comes out clean.
9. Once done, immediately invert the cake onto a serving plate. Let it cool before serving.

Nutritional Values: Calories: ~250 kcal per slice, Protein: ~3g, Fat: ~7g, Carbohydrates: ~45g

1950s Trivia: The Pineapple Upside Down Cake saw a surge in popularity in the 1950s when canned pineapples became more available. It became a household favorite for its sweetness, moisture, and attractive appearance.

Classic Root Beer Float

Ingredients:

- Chilled root beer (1 can or bottle)
- Vanilla ice cream (2 scoops)

Preparation:

1. Place two scoops of vanilla ice cream in a tall glass.
2. Slowly pour chilled root beer over the ice cream until the glass is full.
3. Serve immediately with a straw and a long spoon.

Nutritional Values: Calories: ~270 kcal, Protein: ~2g, Fat: ~9g, Carbohydrates: ~45g

1950s Trivia: The root beer float, also known as a "black cow," was a popular treat in soda shops and diners throughout the 1950s. This delightful beverage offered both refreshment and dessert in one glass, epitomizing the fun and indulgence of the era.

Tuna Salad

Ingredients:

- Canned tuna (1 can, drained)
- Chopped celery (1/2 cup)
- Chopped onion (1/4 cup)
- Mayonnaise (1/3 cup)
- Salt and pepper to taste
- Lettuce leaves for serving

Preparation:

1. In a medium bowl, combine the drained tuna, chopped celery, and chopped onion.
2. Add mayonnaise to the mixture and stir until well combined.
3. Season with salt and pepper to taste.
4. Chill the tuna salad in the refrigerator for at least one hour before serving.
5. Serve the tuna salad on lettuce leaves as a refreshing and light meal.

Nutritional Values: Calories: ~200 kcal per serving, Protein: ~15g, Fat: ~12g, Carbohydrates: ~5g

1950s Trivia: Tuna salad became a staple in American households in the 1950s due to its simplicity and the affordability and availability of canned tuna. It was commonly used as a filling for sandwiches or served on a bed of lettuce.

Jell-O Salad

Ingredients:

- Lemon or lime Jell-O (1 packet)
- Boiling water (1 cup)
- Cold water (1 cup)
- Canned fruit cocktail (1 cup, drained)
- Whipped cream for topping (optional)

Preparation:

1. Dissolve the Jell-O in boiling water, stirring until completely dissolved.
2. Stir in cold water and let it cool slightly.
3. Add the drained fruit cocktail to the Jell-O mixture.
4. Pour into a mold or individual serving dishes.
5. Chill in the refrigerator until set, usually for at least 4 hours or overnight.
6. Unmold the Jell-O salad onto a serving plate and top with whipped cream if desired.

Nutritional Values: Calories: ~100 kcal per serving, Protein: ~2g, Fat: ~0g, Carbohydrates: ~25g

1950s Trivia: Jell-O salads were a quintessential dish in the 1950s, adorning tables at parties and family gatherings. The colorful, jiggly, and fruity dessert represents the era's fascination with modern convenience and aesthetic presentation.

Creamed Chipped Beef on Toast

Ingredients:

- Dried beef slices (2 oz)
- Butter (2 tbsp)
- All-purpose flour (2 tbsp)
- Milk (1 1/2 cups)
- Toasted bread slices
- Salt and pepper to taste

Preparation:

1. Melt the butter in a saucepan over medium heat.
2. Stir in the flour until smooth and cook for about a minute.
3. Gradually whisk in the milk and cook, stirring continuously, until thickened.
4. Add the dried beef slices to the sauce and stir until heated through.
5. Season with salt and pepper to taste.
6. Serve the creamy beef mixture over toasted bread slices.

Nutritional Values: Calories: ~300 kcal per serving, Protein: ~15g, Fat: ~15g, Carbohydrates: ~25g

1950s Trivia: Creamed chipped beef on toast, also known as "S.O.S," was a comforting and economical dish popular in the 1950s. The recipe's simplicity and heartiness made it a favorite among families during this decade.

Banana Split

Ingredients:

- Bananas (1, split lengthwise)
- Vanilla ice cream (1 scoop)
- Chocolate syrup (2 tbsp)
- Whipped cream
- Chopped nuts
- Maraschino cherry

Preparation:

1. Place the split banana in a dish.
2. Top with a scoop of vanilla ice cream.
3. Drizzle chocolate syrup over the ice cream.
4. Add a dollop of whipped cream on top.
5. Sprinkle with chopped nuts and garnish with a maraschino cherry.

Nutritional Values: Calories: ~350 kcal, Protein: ~4g, Fat: ~15g, Carbohydrates: ~55g

1950s Trivia: Banana splits, with their colorful and delightful presentation, were a popular choice for a treat in the 1950s. They were commonly enjoyed at soda fountains and ice cream parlors.

Pimiento Cheese Spread

Ingredients:

- Grated sharp cheddar cheese (2 cups)
- Diced pimientos (1 jar, drained)
- Mayonnaise (1/2 cup)
- Salt and pepper to taste

Preparation:

1. In a bowl, combine the grated cheese, diced pimientos, and mayonnaise.
2. Mix until well combined, and season with salt and pepper to taste.
3. Chill the spread in the refrigerator and serve with crackers or vegetable sticks.

Nutritional Values: Calories: ~150 kcal per serving, Protein: ~5g, Fat: ~12g, Carbohydrates: ~2g

1950s Trivia: Pimiento cheese spread was a staple in American households in the 1950s, enjoyed as a dip or sandwich filling for its creamy texture and savory flavor.

Pinwheel Sandwiches

Ingredients:

- White bread slices (2, crusts removed)
- Cream cheese (2 tbsp)
- Sliced ham or turkey (2 slices)
- Lettuce leaf

Preparation:

1. Flatten the bread slices with a rolling pin.
2. Spread cream cheese over each slice.
3. Place a slice of ham or turkey on top of the cream cheese.
4. Roll up the bread slices tightly.
5. Cut into pinwheels and serve with a lettuce leaf.

Nutritional Values: Calories: ~200 kcal per serving, Protein: ~10g, Fat: ~10g, Carbohydrates: ~20g

1950s Trivia: Pinwheel sandwiches were a delightful and fashionable snack in the 1950s. They were often served at parties and gatherings and were popular for their visual appeal and easy-to-eat form.

Classic Milkshake

Ingredients:

- Vanilla ice cream (2 scoops)
- Whole milk (1 cup)
- Sugar (2 tbsp)
- Vanilla extract (1 tsp)

Preparation:

1. Combine all ingredients in a blender.
2. Blend until smooth and creamy.
3. Pour into a tall glass and serve with a straw.

Nutritional Values: Calories: ~400 kcal per serving, Protein: ~8g, Fat: ~18g, Carbohydrates: ~50g

1950s Trivia: Milkshakes were a quintessential 1950s snack, enjoyed by individuals of all ages. Soda fountains and diners commonly served these thick and creamy treats, often accompanying burgers and fries.

Cheese Ball with Crackers

Ingredients:

- Cream cheese (8 oz)
- Grated cheddar cheese (1 cup)
- Chopped nuts (1/2 cup)
- Chopped chives or green onions (2 tbsp)
- Salt and pepper to taste
- Crackers for serving

Preparation:

1. In a bowl, mix together cream cheese, cheddar cheese, and chives or green onions.
2. Form the mixture into a ball.
3. Roll the ball in chopped nuts until covered.
4. Chill in the refrigerator and serve with crackers.

Nutritional Values: Calories: ~200 kcal per serving, Protein: ~7g, Fat: ~16g, Carbohydrates: ~6g

1950s Trivia: Cheese balls were a popular snack and appetizer in the 1950s, often gracing the tables at parties, holidays, and events. They were loved for their rich flavor and ease of preparation.

Peanut Butter & Jelly Sandwich

Ingredients:

- Sliced bread (2 slices)
- Peanut butter (2 tbsp)
- Jelly or jam (1 tbsp)

Preparation:

1. Spread peanut butter on one slice of bread and jelly or jam on the other.
2. Press the two slices together to form a sandwich.

Nutritional Values: Calories: ~350 kcal per serving, Protein: ~12g, Fat: ~18g, Carbohydrates: ~35g

1950s Trivia: The peanut butter and jelly sandwich is a timeless American snack. In the 1950s, it was a favorite choice for a quick, satisfying bite, often enjoyed by children and adults alike.

Celery Sticks with Cream Cheese

Ingredients:

- Celery stalks
- Cream cheese (1 tbsp per stalk)
- Paprika (optional)

Preparation:

1. Wash and cut the celery stalks into 3-4 inch pieces.
2. Fill the groove of each celery piece with cream cheese.
3. Sprinkle with paprika for extra flavor if desired.

Nutritional Values: Calories: ~50 kcal per serving, Protein: ~1g, Fat: ~4g, Carbohydrates: ~2g

1950s Trivia: Celery sticks filled with cream cheese were a popular healthy and crunchy snack in the 1950s, often served at parties and gatherings as a refreshing appetizer.

Fruit Salad Cup

Ingredients:

- Mixed fresh fruits (1 cup, diced)
- Honey or syrup (2 tbsp)

Preparation:

1. Combine the mixed fresh fruits in a bowl.
2. Drizzle with honey or syrup and toss gently to combine.
3. Serve chilled in individual cups.

Nutritional Values: Calories: ~100 kcal per serving, Protein: ~1g, Fat: ~0g, Carbohydrates: ~25g

1950s Trivia: Fruit salads, served in individual cups, were a refreshing and healthy snack choice, often seen on the tables at parties and gatherings.

Banana Pancakes

Ingredients:

- All-purpose flour (1 cup)
- Baking powder (2 tsp)
- Salt (1/2 tsp)
- Sugar (2 tbsp)
- Egg (1, beaten)
- Milk (3/4 cup)
- Ripe bananas (2, mashed)
- Butter (for greasing the pan)

Preparation:

1. In a large mixing bowl, sift together the flour, baking powder, and salt. Stir in the sugar.
2. In another bowl, combine the beaten egg, milk, and mashed bananas.
3. Add the wet ingredients to the dry ingredients and stir until just combined. It's okay if the batter is a bit lumpy.
4. Heat a griddle or frying pan over medium heat and lightly grease it with butter.
5. Pour about 1/4 cup of the batter onto the griddle for each pancake.
6. Cook until bubbles appear on the surface of the pancake and the edges look set, about 2-3 minutes.
7. Flip the pancake and cook for another 2-3 minutes on the other side, or until golden brown.
8. Remove from the griddle and keep warm. Repeat with the remaining batter.
9. Serve the banana pancakes hot with butter, syrup, or additional sliced bananas on top.

Nutritional Values: Calories: ~250 kcal per serving, Protein: ~6g, Fat: ~3g, Carbohydrates: ~50g

1950s Trivia: In the 1950s, bananas became a popular fruit to incorporate into various dishes, including pancakes. This was in part due to the increased availability and affordability of bananas post-World War II. This era also saw a trend of convenient and quick-to-prepare meals, and pancakes were a favorite choice for a delightful and easy-to-make breakfast or snack.

Enjoy your banana pancakes with a touch of nostalgia!

Bacon, Eggs, and Toast

Ingredients:

- Bacon strips (4 pieces)
- Eggs (2)
- Bread slices (2)
- Butter
- Salt and pepper to taste

Preparation:

1. Lay the bacon strips on a cold skillet and place over medium heat. Cook, turning occasionally, until crispy and golden brown (about 4-6 minutes each side). Place the cooked bacon on a plate lined with paper towels.
2. In the same skillet, crack and cook the eggs over medium heat to your preference (for sunny-side up, let them cook until the whites are set and yolk is still runny, about 2-3 minutes). Season with salt and pepper.
3. Butter both sides of the bread slices and toast in a toaster until golden and crispy. If no toaster is available, use the oven broiler or another skillet over medium heat.
4. Arrange the cooked bacon, eggs, and toast on a plate and serve immediately.

Nutritional Values: Calories: ~450 kcal per serving, Protein: ~20g, Fat: ~30g, Carbohydrates: ~25g

1950s Trivia: The "Bacon, Eggs, and Toast" breakfast was considered a wholesome and hearty start to the day in the 1950s. Families enjoying post-war prosperity consumed more meat, making bacon a popular choice for a satisfying breakfast, paired perfectly with eggs and toast for a balanced meal.

Porridge with Fresh Milk

Ingredients:

- Rolled oats (1 cup)
- Fresh milk (2 cups)
- Salt (a pinch)
- Sugar or honey (to taste)
- Fresh fruits or nuts for topping (optional)

Preparation:

1. In a saucepan, combine the rolled oats, one cup of fresh milk, and a pinch of salt.
2. Place the saucepan over medium heat and bring the mixture to a simmer. Cook, stirring frequently, for 5-7 minutes or until the oats are tender and the porridge is thickened to your liking.
3. Remove the saucepan from the heat and let the porridge sit for a few minutes to thicken further.
4. Pour the porridge into a bowl and drizzle with the remaining fresh milk. Sweeten with sugar or honey to taste.
5. If desired, top the porridge with fresh fruits or nuts for added flavor and nutrition.

Nutritional Values: Calories: ~300 kcal per serving, Protein: ~10g, Fat: ~7g, Carbohydrates: ~50g

1950s Trivia: In the 1950s, porridge was a common breakfast item, especially during the colder months. It was seen as a warm, filling, and nutritious start to the day. Preparing it with fresh milk added richness and nutritional value, and toppings like fresh fruits or nuts were often used to enhance the flavor and provide additional health benefits.

Blueberry Pancakes

Ingredients:

- All-purpose flour (1 cup)
- Baking powder (1 tsp)
- Salt (1/2 tsp)
- Sugar (2 tbsp)
- Egg (1, beaten)
- Milk (3/4 cup)
- Fresh blueberries (1 cup)
- Butter or oil (for greasing the pan)

Preparation:

1. In a large bowl, sift together the flour, baking powder, and salt. Add the sugar and mix well.
2. In another bowl, combine the beaten egg and milk.
3. Add the wet ingredients to the dry ingredients and stir until just combined. The batter should be slightly lumpy.
4. Gently fold in the fresh blueberries.
5. Heat a griddle or frying pan over medium heat and lightly grease it with butter or oil.
6. Pour about 1/4 cup of the batter onto the griddle for each pancake. Cook until bubbles appear on the surface and the edges look set, about 2-3 minutes.
7. Flip the pancakes and cook on the other side for an additional 2-3 minutes or until golden brown.
8. Serve the blueberry pancakes hot with butter, syrup, or additional blueberries.

Nutritional Values: Calories: ~250 kcal per serving, Protein: ~6g, Fat: ~4g, Carbohydrates: ~45g

1950s Trivia: Blueberry pancakes were a beloved breakfast dish in the 1950s, offering a sweet and satisfying start to the day. As blueberries became more widely available, they were often incorporated into pancakes for their delightful burst of flavor and vibrant color. Served hot off the griddle with a pat of butter and a drizzle of syrup, blueberry pancakes were a surefire way to bring the family together around the breakfast table.

Breakfast Steak

Ingredients:

- Beef steak (sirloin or ribeye, 6-8 oz)
- Salt (to taste)
- Black pepper (to taste)
- Olive oil or butter (1 tbsp)
- Garlic (1 clove, minced, optional)
- Fresh thyme or rosemary (optional)

Preparation:

1. Allow the steak to come to room temperature for about 30 minutes before cooking.
2. Season the steak generously with salt and pepper on both sides.
3. Heat a skillet over medium-high heat and add olive oil or butter.
4. Once hot, add the steak to the skillet. If using, add minced garlic and fresh herbs for additional flavor.
5. Cook the steak for 3-4 minutes on each side for medium-rare, or until it reaches your desired level of doneness.
6. Remove the steak from the skillet and let it rest for a few minutes before serving.

Nutritional Values: Calories: ~300 kcal per serving, Protein: ~22g, Fat: ~23g, Carbohydrates: ~0g

1950s Trivia: In the 1950s, the idea of a protein-rich, hearty breakfast gained popularity, especially among working individuals who needed sustained energy throughout the day. Breakfast steak, therefore, became a sought-after morning meal, providing ample protein and satiety. This dish was often paired with eggs, toast, or other breakfast staples to create a comprehensive, energizing meal to start the day.

Cheese Sandwiches

Ingredients:

- Bread slices (2 per sandwich)
- Cheddar cheese (2 slices per sandwich)
- Butter (as needed)
- Optional additional ingredients: tomato slices, cooked bacon strips, lettuce

Preparation:

1. Lay out the bread slices and place the cheddar cheese on one slice for each sandwich. Add any additional ingredients you desire.
2. Top with the second bread slice to form sandwiches.
3. Butter the outside of the bread slices.
4. Heat a skillet or sandwich grill over medium heat.
5. Place the sandwiches in the skillet or on the grill, and cook until the bread is toasted golden brown and the cheese is melted, about 3-4 minutes on each side.
6. Remove from heat and serve the cheese sandwiches hot.

Nutritional Values: Calories: ~350 kcal per serving, Protein: ~15g, Fat: ~20g, Carbohydrates: ~25g

1950s Trivia: The cheese sandwich, simple and versatile, was a classic choice for a quick and easy meal in the 1950s. It could be enjoyed at any time of the day, including breakfast or as a snack. In post-war America, with the advent of processed foods, pre-sliced bread and cheese made such sandwiches convenient and popular. Families in the 1950s often enjoyed them with a cup of hot soup or a side of chips, making for a satisfying and effortless meal.

Avocado and Crab Salad

Ingredients:

- 1 ripe avocado
- 1 cup cooked and shredded crab meat
- 1/4 cup mayonnaise
- 1 tsp lemon juice
- Salt and pepper to taste

Preparation:

1. Cut the avocado in half and remove the pit.
2. In a bowl, mix the crab meat, mayonnaise, and lemon juice. Season with salt and pepper.
3. Fill the avocado halves with the crab mixture.
4. Serve chilled.

Fun Fact:

In the 1950s, avocados became a popular food item in the United States, and combining them with seafood, like crab, became a fashionable snack or light meal.

Tomato Soup with Grilled Cheese Dipper

Ingredients:

- 1 can condensed tomato soup
- 1 can of water or milk
- 2 slices of bread
- 2 slices of cheddar cheese
- 2 tbsp butter

Preparation:

1. Heat the tomato soup and water or milk in a saucepan over medium heat.
2. While the soup is heating, make a grilled cheese sandwich: butter the bread slices and place the cheese between them.
3. Cook the sandwich in a skillet over medium heat until the bread is toasted and the cheese is melted.
4. Cut the sandwich into strips and serve with the hot tomato soup for dipping.

Fun Fact:

Tomato soup with a grilled cheese sandwich was a comforting and economical meal that gained popularity during the 1950s, especially among children.

Chicken Salad Sandwich

Ingredients:

- 1 cup cooked, shredded chicken
- 1/3 cup chopped celery
- 1/4 cup mayonnaise
- 1 tbsp chopped fresh parsley
- Salt and pepper to taste
- Lettuce leaves
- 2 slices of bread

Preparation:

1. In a bowl, combine chicken, celery, mayonnaise, and parsley. Season with salt and pepper.
2. Spread the mixture on a slice of bread.
3. Top with lettuce and the other bread slice.
4. Cut in half and serve.

Fun Fact:

Chicken Salad Sandwiches became a popular lunch option in the 1950s, often served at luncheons and picnics.

Fruit and Cottage Cheese Plate

Ingredients:

- 1 cup cottage cheese
- 1/2 cup assorted fresh fruit (e.g., pineapple chunks, strawberry halves, and apple slices)
- 1 tbsp honey

Preparation:

1. Place the cottage cheese in the center of a plate.
2. Arrange the fresh fruit around the cottage cheese.
3. Drizzle honey over the fruit and cottage cheese before serving.

Fun Fact:

The Fruit and Cottage Cheese Plate became popular in the 1950s as a light and healthy snack or meal, often enjoyed during the summer months.

Egg Salad Sandwich

Ingredients:

- 4 boiled eggs, chopped
- 1/4 cup mayonnaise
- 1 tbsp mustard

- Salt and pepper to taste
- Lettuce leaves
- 2 slices of bread

Preparation:

1. In a bowl, mix the chopped eggs, mayonnaise, and mustard. Season with salt and pepper.
2. Lay lettuce leaves on a slice of bread.
3. Spread the egg salad over the lettuce.
4. Top with the second bread slice, cut in half, and serve.

Fun Fact:

The Egg Salad Sandwich was a typical 1950s snack, often packed in lunches for both children and adults.

Waldorf Salad

Ingredients:

- 1 cup chopped apples
- 1 cup chopped celery
- 1/2 cup chopped walnuts
- 1/2 cup mayonnaise
- Lettuce leaves

Preparation:

1. Combine apples, celery, and walnuts in a bowl.
2. Mix in the mayonnaise until all ingredients are coated.
3. Serve on a bed of lettuce leaves.

Clam Chowder

Ingredients:

- 2 cans minced clams
- 1 cup chopped onions
- 1 cup chopped celery
- 2 cups diced potatoes
- 3/4 cup melted butter
- 3/4 cup all-purpose flour
- 1 quart half-and-half
- Salt and pepper to taste

Preparation:

1. In a pot, combine clam juice (from the canned clams), onions, celery, and potatoes. Cook until vegetables are tender.
2. In another pot, melt butter and then stir in flour until smooth.
3. Gradually add half-and-half to the butter-flour mixture, stirring constantly until thick.
4. Add the cooked vegetable mixture to the thickened cream mixture. Add minced clams, salt, and pepper. Heat thoroughly and serve.

Fun Fact:

Clam Chowder was a beloved comfort food in the 1950s, especially in the Northeastern United States.

Malt Milkshake

Ingredients:

- 2 scoops vanilla ice cream
- 1/2 cup milk
- 2 tbsp malted milk powder
- Whipped cream (optional)

Preparation:

1. Combine ice cream, milk, and malted milk powder in a blender.
2. Blend until smooth and frothy.
3. Pour into a glass and top with whipped cream if desired.

Fun Fact:

Malt shops were a popular gathering place for teenagers in the 1950s, and malted milkshakes were a favorite treat.

Chicken a la King

Ingredients:

- 2 cups cooked chicken, chopped
- 1 cup mushrooms, sliced
- 1/4 cup butter
- 1/4 cup all-purpose flour
- 1 cup chicken broth
- 1 cup heavy cream
- Salt and pepper to taste

Preparation:

1. In a pan, sauté mushrooms in butter until tender.

2. Stir in flour until blended. Gradually add chicken broth and cream.
3. Bring to a boil, stirring constantly until thickened.
4. Add chopped chicken, salt, and pepper. Heat through and serve over toast or biscuits.

Fun Fact:

Chicken a la King was a popular dish in the 1950s, often served at dinner parties and special gatherings.

Melon Ball Cocktail

Ingredients:

- 1 cup melon balls (cantaloupe, watermelon, honeydew)
- 1/2 cup ginger ale
- Mint leaves for garnish

Preparation:

1. Place melon balls in a glass.
2. Pour ginger ale over the melon balls.
3. Garnish with mint leaves and serve chilled.

Fun Fact:

Melon Ball Cocktail, a refreshing fruit drink, was a trendy choice in the 1950s during summer parties and gatherings.

Enjoy these classic 1950s recipes!

Tomato Aspic

Ingredients:

- 2 cups tomato juice
- 1 tbsp gelatin
- 2 tbsp cold water
- Salt, pepper, and herbs to taste

Preparation:

1. Dissolve gelatin in cold water.
2. Heat tomato juice, but do not boil.
3. Add dissolved gelatin to tomato juice. Stir until completely dissolved.
4. Add salt, pepper, and herbs to taste.
5. Pour into molds and chill until set.

Fun Fact:

In the 1950s, aspics were a trendy dish, often seen at potlucks and parties, showcasing the era's fascination with gelatin.

French Toast

Ingredients:

- 4 slices of bread
- 2 eggs
- 1/2 cup milk
- 1 tsp vanilla extract
- Butter
- Maple syrup

Preparation:

1. Whisk together eggs, milk, and vanilla extract.
2. Dip each slice of bread into the egg mixture, ensuring both sides are coated.
3. Melt butter in a frying pan over medium heat.
4. Fry each side of the soaked bread until golden brown.
5. Serve hot with butter and maple syrup.

Fun Fact:

In the 1950s, French Toast was a popular breakfast item in American diners, often enjoyed with a side of crispy bacon.

Fried Chicken Sandwich

Ingredients:

- Chicken breast
- Flour
- Eggs
- Bread crumbs
- Oil for frying
- Lettuce
- Mayonnaise
- Bread buns

Preparation:

1. Dredge chicken breast in flour, dip in beaten eggs, and then coat with bread crumbs.
2. Fry in hot oil until golden and cooked through.
3. Place the fried chicken on a bun with lettuce and mayonnaise.

Fun Fact:

The fried chicken sandwich, a simple yet satisfying meal, was a quick
and easy option for on-the-go meals during the busy post-war era.

Rice Krispies Treats

Ingredients:

- 3 tbsp butter
- 4 cups mini marshmallows
- 6 cups Rice Krispies cereal

Preparation:

1. Melt butter in a large saucepan.
2. Add marshmallows and stir until melted.
3. Remove from heat and stir in Rice Krispies cereal until well
   coated.
4. Press the mixture into a greased pan and let cool. Cut into
   squares.

Fun Fact:

Rice Krispies Treats were invented in the 1930s but gained significant
popularity in the 1950s as an easy and delicious snack.

Iced Coffee

Ingredients:

- 1 cup brewed coffee, cooled
- Ice cubes
- Milk or cream
- Sugar to taste

Preparation:

1. Fill a glass with ice cubes.
2. Pour cooled coffee over the ice.
3. Add milk or cream and sugar to taste. Stir and enjoy.

Fun Fact:

Iced coffee began to gain traction in the 1950s as more sophisticated refrigeration allowed for more experimentation with cold drinks.

Main Dishes

Meatloaf

Ingredients:

- Ground beef (2 lbs)
- Egg (1)
- Bread crumbs (1 cup)
- Onion (1, finely chopped)
- Ketchup (1/2 cup)
- Mustard (1 tbsp)
- Brown sugar (2 tbsp)
- Salt and pepper to taste

Preparation:

1. Preheat your oven to 375°F (190°C).
2. In a large bowl, mix together the ground beef, egg, bread crumbs, and onion. Season with salt and pepper.
3. Form the mixture into a loaf shape and place it in a baking dish.
4. In a small bowl, mix together the ketchup, mustard, and brown sugar. Spread this mixture over the top of the meatloaf.
5. Bake in the preheated oven for 1 hour or until the meatloaf is cooked through.

Nutritional Values: Calories: ~350 kcal per serving, Protein: ~25g, Fat: ~20g, Carbohydrates: ~15g

1950s Trivia: Meatloaf was a quintessential American dish in the 1950s, symbolizing home-cooked comfort food that was easy to make, economical, and satisfying. Many families had their own beloved meatloaf recipes, often passed down through generations.

Chicken a la King II

Ingredients:

- Cooked chicken (2 cups, diced)
- Butter (1/4 cup)
- Green bell pepper (1, chopped)
- Mushrooms (1 cup, sliced)
- All-purpose flour (1/4 cup)
- Chicken broth (1 cup)
- Heavy cream (1 cup)
- Salt and pepper to taste

Preparation:

1. In a large skillet, melt the butter over medium heat. Add the green bell pepper and mushrooms and sauté until softened.
2. Stir in the flour until the vegetables are coated.
3. Gradually add the chicken broth and heavy cream, stirring constantly until the sauce thickens.
4. Add the diced cooked chicken and cook until heated through. Season with salt and pepper.
5. Serve the Chicken a la King over rice, pasta, or toast.

Nutritional Values: Calories: ~400 kcal per serving, Protein: ~25g, Fat: ~30g, Carbohydrates: ~10g

1950s Trivia: Chicken a la King was a popular dish in the 1950s, often served at dinner parties and special gatherings. It was considered a fancy dish despite its simple ingredients, and was loved for its creamy, comforting flavors.

Tuna Noodle Casserole

Ingredients:

- Egg noodles (3 cups)
- Canned tuna (2 cans, drained)
- Cream of mushroom soup (1 can)
- Frozen peas (1 cup)
- Cheddar cheese (1 cup, shredded)
- Salt and pepper to taste

Preparation:

1. Preheat your oven to 375°F (190°C).
2. Cook the egg noodles according to the package instructions.
3. In a large bowl, combine the cooked noodles, drained tuna, cream of mushroom soup, and frozen peas. Mix until evenly combined.
4. Transfer the mixture to a baking dish and top with shredded cheddar cheese.
5. Bake in the preheated oven for 25-30 minutes or until hot and bubbly.

Nutritional Values: Calories: ~350 kcal per serving, Protein: ~20g, Fat: ~15g, Carbohydrates: ~30g

1950s Trivia: Tuna Noodle Casserole was a staple in many American homes in the 1950s. Its popularity stemmed from its use of convenient canned ingredients, making it a quick and easy dinner option for busy families.

Spaghetti and Meatballs

Ingredients:

- Ground beef (1 lb)
- Bread crumbs (1/2 cup)
- Egg (1)
- Garlic (2 cloves, minced)
- Onion (1, finely chopped)
- Canned tomato sauce (2 cups)
- Spaghetti (1 lb)
- Olive oil (2 tbsp)
- Salt, pepper, and Italian herbs to taste

Preparation:

1. In a bowl, combine the ground beef, bread crumbs, egg, half the garlic, half the onion, salt, and pepper. Form into small meatballs.
2. In a skillet, heat the olive oil over medium heat. Add the meatballs and cook until browned on all sides.
3. Remove the meatballs and in the same skillet, sauté the remaining garlic and onion until softened.
4. Add the tomato sauce and Italian herbs to the skillet, and then return the meatballs to the sauce. Simmer for about 30 minutes.
5. While the sauce simmers, cook the spaghetti according to package instructions.
6. Serve the meatballs and sauce over the cooked spaghetti.

Nutritional Values: Calories: ~550 kcal per serving, Protein: ~25g, Fat: ~25g, Carbohydrates: ~60g

1950s Trivia: Spaghetti and Meatballs was a beloved dish in the 1950s in America, particularly among Italian-American communities. This dish represented a merging of Italian culinary traditions with American sensibilities, creating a comforting and hearty meal that was enjoyed by many families across the country.

Chicken-Fried Steak

Ingredients:

- Cube steak (4 pieces)
- All-purpose flour (1 cup)
- Egg (1, beaten)
- Milk (1 cup)
- Oil for frying
- Salt and pepper to taste

Preparation:

1. Season the cube steaks with salt and pepper.
2. Dredge the steaks in flour, then dip in the beaten egg, and dredge in flour again.
3. Heat oil in a large skillet over medium-high heat. Fry the steaks until golden brown and cooked through, about 4 minutes per side.
4. Remove the steaks and drain on paper towels. Serve with milk gravy made from the drippings.

Nutritional Values: Calories: ~450 kcal per serving, Protein: ~30g, Fat: ~30g, Carbohydrates: ~15g

1950s Trivia: Chicken-fried steak was another comfort food classic from the 1950s, especially in the Southern United States. It was a symbol of homestyle cooking and often served with sides like mashed potatoes and green beans for a filling and satisfying meal.

Baked Alaska

Ingredients:

- Sponge cake or brownie layer (1)
- Ice cream (1 quart, softened)
- Egg whites (4)
- Sugar (3/4 cup)

Preparation:

1. Line a bowl with plastic wrap and fill with softened ice cream. Refreeze until hard.
2. Preheat your oven broiler.
3. Place the sponge cake or brownie layer on a baking sheet. Unmold the ice cream on top.
4. In a bowl, beat the egg whites until soft peaks form. Gradually add the sugar, beating until stiff and glossy.
5. Spread the meringue over the ice cream and cake, sealing the edges.
6. Place under the broiler until the meringue is golden brown. Serve immediately.

Nutritional Values: Calories: ~350 kcal per serving, Protein: ~5g, Fat: ~15g, Carbohydrates: ~50g

1950s Trivia: Baked Alaska became a popular dessert in fancy restaurants during the 1950s. It was considered a special-occasion dessert due to its dramatic presentation, with the contrast between the hot meringue and the cold ice cream providing a delightful experience for the diner.

Tomato Bisque

Ingredients:

- Ripe tomatoes, 6 (medium-sized, diced) or 1 can (28 oz.) of diced tomatoes
- Chicken or vegetable broth, 2 cups
- Heavy cream, 1 cup
- Onion, 1 (medium-sized, finely chopped)
- Garlic, 2 cloves (minced)
- Unsalted butter, 4 tablespoons
- Sugar, 1 tablespoon
- Salt and pepper, to taste
- Fresh basil or parsley, for garnish (optional)
- Toasted croutons, for serving (optional)

Directions:

1. In a large pot, melt the butter over medium heat. Add the finely chopped onions and sauté until translucent, about 4-5 minutes.
2. Add the minced garlic and sauté for another minute until fragrant.
3. Pour in the diced tomatoes (with their juices) and the chicken or vegetable broth. Bring the mixture to a simmer.
4. Once simmering, reduce the heat and let the soup cook for about 20 minutes, stirring occasionally.
5. Use an immersion blender or a standard blender (in batches) to puree the soup until it's smooth.
6. Return the soup to the pot (if using a standard blender) and stir in the heavy cream. Add the sugar and season with salt and pepper to taste. Warm the soup over low heat until it's heated through.
7. Serve the tomato bisque in bowls, garnished with fresh basil or parsley if desired. Toasted croutons can be added on top for some crunch.

1950s Fact: While Clam Chowder was a favorite along the coastal regions, Tomato Bisque found its way to many American tables during the 1950s, especially with the rise of canned goods. Creamy and rich, this soup was often paired with a classic grilled cheese sandwich for a comforting meal.

Lobster Newberg

Ingredients:

- Cooked lobster meat (2 cups, chopped)
- Egg yolks (4)
- Brandy (2 tbsp)
- Heavy cream (1 cup)
- Butter (4 tbsp)
- Salt, paprika, and cayenne pepper to taste

Preparation:

1. In a skillet, melt the butter and add the lobster meat. Cook until heated through.
2. In a bowl, beat together the egg yolks, brandy, and heavy cream.
3. Stir the egg mixture into the skillet with the lobster, and cook over low heat until the sauce thickens. Season with salt, paprika, and cayenne pepper.
4. Serve the Lobster Newberg over buttered toast or in a puff pastry shell.

Nutritional Values: Calories: ~400 kcal per serving, Protein: ~20g, Fat: ~30g, Carbohydrates: ~5g

1950s Trivia: Lobster Newberg was a luxurious dish enjoyed in upscale restaurants during the 1950s. It was often ordered for special occasions and celebrations, symbolizing elegance and sophistication in American dining.

Chicken Tetrazzini

Ingredients:

- Cooked spaghetti, 8 oz.
- Cooked chicken, 2 cups (diced or shredded)
- Mushrooms, 1 cup (sliced)
- Butter, 4 tbsp.
- Flour, 2 tbsp.
- Chicken broth, 2 cups
- Cream, 1 cup
- Grated Parmesan cheese, 1/2 cup
- Sherry, 2 tbsp. (optional)
- Almonds, 1/4 cup (sliced)
- Bread crumbs, 1/4 cup
- Salt and pepper, to taste

Directions:

1. Preheat the oven to 375°F (190°C).
2. In a large saucepan, melt the butter over medium heat. Add the mushrooms and sauté until they begin to soften.
3. Stir in the flour, ensuring the mushrooms are coated. Gradually add the chicken broth and cream, stirring continuously until the mixture thickens.
4. Remove from heat and stir in the sherry, if using. Season with salt and pepper to taste.
5. In a greased baking dish, layer the cooked spaghetti, followed by the cooked chicken.
6. Pour the creamy mushroom sauce over the chicken and spaghetti. Ensure everything is well-coated.
7. Sprinkle with grated Parmesan cheese, breadcrumbs, and sliced almonds.
8. Bake in the preheated oven for about 25-30 minutes or until the top is golden brown and bubbly.

9. Remove from the oven and let sit for a few minutes before
    serving.

1950s Fact: Named after the Italian opera singer Luisa Tetrazzini,
Chicken Tetrazzini was a beloved potluck dish, making regular
appearances at family dinners in the '50s. Its creamy texture and rich
flavor made it an instant classic in American households.

Salmon Loaf

Ingredients:

- Canned salmon, 1 lb. (drained and flaked)
- Fresh breadcrumbs, 1 cup
- Onion, 1 (finely chopped)
- Celery, 2 stalks (finely chopped)
- Fresh parsley, 1/4 cup (chopped)
- Eggs, 2 (beaten)
- Whole milk, 1/2 cup
- Lemon juice, 1 tbsp.
- Salt and pepper, to taste
- Butter or margarine, 2 tbsp. (melted)

Directions:

1. Preheat oven to 350°F (175°C).
2. In a mixing bowl, combine the flaked salmon, breadcrumbs,
    onion, celery, parsley, eggs, milk, lemon juice, melted butter,
    salt, and pepper. Mix until well combined.
3. Transfer the mixture to a loaf pan, pressing it down firmly.
4. Bake in the preheated oven for 45-50 minutes, or until the top
    turns golden brown.
5. Let the salmon loaf cool for a few minutes before removing
    from the pan and slicing.
6. Serve warm with tartar sauce or a lemon wedge on the side.

Ham and Noodle Casserole

Ingredients:

- Wide egg noodles, 2 cups (cooked)
- Cooked ham, 2 cups (diced)
- Canned cream of mushroom soup, 1 can
- Sour cream, 1 cup
- Grated sharp cheddar cheese, 1 cup
- Frozen peas, 1 cup (thawed)
- Salt and pepper, to taste
- Breadcrumbs, 1/2 cup
- Butter, 2 tbsp. (melted)

Directions:

1. Preheat oven to 375°F (190°C).
2. In a large mixing bowl, combine the cooked noodles, diced ham, mushroom soup, sour cream, cheese, and peas. Mix until well combined. Season with salt and pepper to taste.
3. Transfer the mixture to a greased casserole dish.
4. In a small bowl, mix the breadcrumbs with melted butter. Sprinkle this mixture over the casserole.
5. Bake in the preheated oven for 25-30 minutes, or until bubbly and golden brown on top.
6. Remove from oven and allow to cool slightly before serving.

1950s Fact: Casseroles were a popular dish in the 1950s as they were both budget-friendly and could feed a large family. Using leftover ham or other meats in casseroles was a common practice.

Shrimp à la Creole

Ingredients:

- Medium-sized shrimp, 1 lb, peeled and deveined
- Onion, 1 (medium, finely chopped)
- Green bell pepper, 1 (finely chopped)
- Garlic cloves, 2 (minced)
- Canned tomatoes, 1 cup (chopped)
- Tomato paste, 2 tbsp
- Bay leaf, 1
- Worcestershire sauce, 1 tsp
- Tabasco sauce, a few drops (to taste)
- White wine, 1/4 cup
- Butter, 2 tbsp
- Salt and pepper, to taste
- Fresh parsley, for garnish (chopped)

Directions:

1. In a large skillet, melt butter over medium heat. Add onions, green bell pepper, and garlic. Sauté until translucent.
2. Add the chopped tomatoes, tomato paste, bay leaf, Worcestershire sauce, and Tabasco sauce to the skillet. Stir and cook for 5 minutes.
3. Pour in the white wine and allow it to simmer for an additional 3 minutes.

4. Add the shrimp to the skillet, ensuring they are well-covered by the sauce. Cook until the shrimp are pink and fully cooked, about 5 minutes.
5. Season with salt and pepper to taste.
6. Discard the bay leaf.
7. Serve the Shrimp à la Creole over steamed white rice and garnish with fresh parsley.

1950s Fact: Seafood dishes were a lavish treat in many 1950s households. As transportation improved, ingredients like shrimp became more accessible, leading to an influx of recipes that spotlighted these delectable treats. Shrimp à la Creole with its rich, spicy tomato sauce was a favorite in Southern American households and was often served at dinner parties and special occasions.

Chicken Fried Steak

Ingredients:

- Cube steak (4 pieces)
- Flour (1 cup)
- Eggs (2, beaten)
- Bread crumbs (1 cup)
- Oil for frying
- Salt and pepper to taste

Preparation:

1. Season the cube steak with salt and pepper.
2. Dredge each piece in flour, then dip in beaten eggs, and coat with bread crumbs.
3. Heat oil in a skillet and fry the coated steaks until they are golden brown and cooked through.

4. Drain on paper towels and serve with gravy and mashed
    potatoes.

Nutritional Values: Calories: ~400 kcal per serving, Protein: ~30g,
Fat: ~20g, Carbohydrates: ~25g

1950s Trivia: Chicken Fried Steak was a popular dish in the 1950s,
especially in the Southern United States. It represented comfort food at
its finest and was often enjoyed as a hearty dinner meal, showcasing the
simplicity and deliciousness of American home cooking.

Frosted Ribbon Loaf

Ingredients:

- Vanilla ice cream, 1 quart
- Strawberry ice cream, 1 quart
- Chocolate ice cream, 1 quart
- Crushed pineapple, 1 cup (drained)
- Maraschino cherries, 1/2 cup (chopped)
- Whipped cream, 2 cups
- Sliced almonds, 1/2 cup (toasted)

Directions:

1. Allow all three ice cream flavors to soften slightly but not melt.
2. In a 9x5-inch loaf pan, spread vanilla ice cream as the first
    layer. Place the pan in the freezer for about 30 minutes or until
    the layer is firm.
3. Once the vanilla layer is firm, spread the strawberry ice cream
    on top and return to the freezer for another 30 minutes.
4. Combine the crushed pineapple and chopped cherries in a small
    bowl. Once the strawberry layer is firm, spread this fruit mixture
    over it.

5. Top the fruit layer with the chocolate ice cream. Freeze the assembled loaf for at least 6 hours or overnight.
6. Just before serving, take the loaf out of the freezer and invert it onto a serving plate. Spread whipped cream over the entire loaf, and sprinkle with toasted almonds.
7. Slice and serve immediately.

1950s Fact: Ice cream desserts like the Frosted Ribbon Loaf were festive and popular for family gatherings in the 1950s. Using multiple flavors and incorporating fruits made it a delightful treat that was visually appealing as well.

Pineapple-Glazed Ham

Ingredients:

- Bone-in ham (5 lbs)
- Pineapple slices (1 can)
- Brown sugar (1 cup)
- Mustard (2 tbsp)
- Cloves (1 tbsp)

Preparation:

1. Preheat the oven as per the ham's cooking instructions.
2. Score the surface of the ham and stud with cloves.
3. Mix brown sugar and mustard and rub over the ham.
4. Arrange pineapple slices on the ham and secure with toothpicks.
5. Bake according to the ham's cooking instructions, basting occasionally with the juices.

Nutritional Values: Calories: ~400 kcal per serving, Protein: ~35g, Fat: ~20g, Carbohydrates: ~20g

Beef Stroganoff

Ingredients:

- Beef sirloin (1 lb, sliced)
- Mushrooms (1 cup, sliced)
- Onion (1, chopped)
- Beef broth (1 cup)
- Sour cream (1 cup)
- Flour (2 tbsp)
- Butter (2 tbsp)
- Salt and pepper to taste
- Cooked egg noodles for serving

Preparation:

1. In a skillet, melt the butter and brown the beef slices.
2. Remove the beef and sauté the mushrooms and onion in the same skillet.
3. Add the beef back into the skillet, along with the beef broth, and simmer until the beef is tender.
4. Stir in the sour cream and flour, cooking until the sauce thickens.
5. Serve over cooked egg noodles.

Nutritional Values: Calories: ~500 kcal per serving, Protein: ~30g, Fat: ~35g, Carbohydrates: ~20g

Chicken and Rice Casserole

Ingredients:

- Chicken breasts, 4 (boneless and skinless)
- Long-grain white rice, 1 cup (uncooked)
- Canned cream of celery soup, 1 can
- Chicken broth, 2 cups
- Frozen mixed vegetables, 1 cup (thawed)
- Salt and pepper, to taste
- Paprika, for garnish

Directions:

1. Preheat oven to 375°F (190°C).
2. Spread the uncooked rice evenly on the bottom of a greased casserole dish.
3. Place the chicken breasts on top of the rice.
4. In a mixing bowl, combine the cream of celery soup and chicken broth. Pour this mixture over the chicken and rice.
5. Scatter the mixed vegetables around the chicken.
6. Season with salt, pepper, and a sprinkle of paprika.
7. Cover the casserole with aluminum foil.
8. Bake in the preheated oven for 45-50 minutes, or until the chicken is fully cooked and the rice is tender.
9. Allow the casserole to sit for a few minutes before serving.

1950s Fact: The use of canned soups in recipes, like the Chicken and Rice Casserole, was trendy in the 1950s. It allowed for quick meal preparation and added a creamy texture to dishes.

Swedish Meatballs

Ingredients:

- Ground beef, 1/2 lb.
- Ground pork, 1/2 lb.
- Onion, 1 (finely chopped)
- Breadcrumbs, 1/2 cup
- Milk, 1/2 cup
- Eggs, 2
- Nutmeg, 1/4 tsp.
- Allspice, 1/4 tsp.
- Salt and pepper, to taste
- Butter, 2 tbsp.
- Beef broth, 2 cups
- Heavy cream, 1/2 cup

Directions:

1. In a bowl, soak the breadcrumbs in milk for about 5 minutes.
2. Add the ground beef, ground pork, onion, eggs, nutmeg, allspice, salt, and pepper to the breadcrumb mixture. Mix until well combined.
3. Roll the mixture into 1-inch meatballs.
4. In a skillet, melt the butter over medium heat. Add the meatballs and brown them on all sides.
5. Once browned, remove the meatballs and set aside. In the same skillet, pour the beef broth and bring to a simmer.
6. Return the meatballs to the skillet and let them simmer in the broth for about 20 minutes.
7. Add the heavy cream, stir, and cook for another 5 minutes until the sauce thickens slightly.
8. Serve the meatballs with the creamy sauce and garnished with chopped parsley.

Chicken Divan

Ingredients:

- Broccoli, 4 cups (cut into florets and steamed)
- Cooked chicken breasts, 4 (sliced)
- Butter, 4 tbsp.
- Flour, 4 tbsp.
- Chicken broth, 2 cups
- Cream, 1 cup
- Grated Parmesan cheese, 1/2 cup
- Dry white wine or sherry, 1/4 cup (optional)
- Curry powder, 1 tsp.
- Bread crumbs, 1/2 cup
- Cheddar cheese, 1/2 cup (grated)
- Salt and pepper, to taste

Directions:

1. Preheat the oven to 375°F (190°C).
2. Arrange the steamed broccoli in a greased baking dish, followed by the sliced chicken.
3. In a saucepan, melt butter over medium heat. Stir in flour until smooth.
4. Gradually whisk in the chicken broth, followed by the cream, stirring continuously until the mixture thickens.
5. Add the white wine or sherry, if using, along with curry powder, salt, and pepper. Stir well.
6. Pour the sauce over the chicken and broccoli.

7. Sprinkle with grated Parmesan cheese, cheddar cheese, and bread crumbs.
8. Bake in the preheated oven for 25-30 minutes or until the top is golden brown and bubbly.
9. Serve hot, ideally with rice or noodles.

1950s Fact: Chicken Divan originated at the Divan Parisien Restaurant in the Chatham Hotel in New York City in the 1930s. By the 1950s, it had become a popular dish for dinner parties and potlucks due to its easy preparation and elegant presentation.

Chicken and Rice Casserole

Ingredients:

- Chicken pieces (2 lbs)
- White rice (1 cup)
- Cream of chicken soup (1 can)
- Chicken broth (1 cup)
- Onion (1, chopped)
- Paprika, salt, and pepper to taste

Preparation:

1. Preheat the oven to 375°F (190°C).
2. In a baking dish, spread the rice and top with chicken pieces.
3. Mix the soup, chicken broth, and onion, and pour over the chicken and rice.
4. Season with paprika, salt, and pepper.
5. Cover and bake for 1 hour or until the chicken is cooked through and the rice is tender.

Nutritional Values: Calories: ~450 kcal per serving, Protein: ~30g, Fat: ~20g, Carbohydrates: ~30g

1950s Trivia: Chicken and rice casserole was a comfort food classic in the 1950s, often made with the convenience of canned soup. The ease and affordability of this dish made it a household staple, providing a wholesome meal with minimal effort.

Salisbury Steak

Ingredients:

- Ground beef (1 lb)
- Onion soup mix (1 packet)
- Egg (1)
- Bread crumbs (1/2 cup)
- Mushroom gravy (1 can)

Preparation:

1. Preheat the oven to 350°F (175°C).
2. Mix the ground beef, onion soup mix, egg, and bread crumbs.
3. Form into oval patties and place in a baking dish.
4. Pour mushroom gravy over the patties.
5. Bake for 45 minutes or until cooked through.

Nutritional Values: Calories: ~350 kcal per serving, Protein: ~25g, Fat: ~20g, Carbohydrates: ~15g

1950s Trivia: Salisbury steak became popular in the 1950s as a hearty and satisfying meal. Named after an American physician, Dr. Salisbury, who promoted a meat-centered diet, it was an early version of the hamburger without the bun.

Honey-Glazed Corned Beef

Ingredients:

- Corned beef brisket, 3-4 lbs
- Whole grain mustard, 1/4 cup
- Honey, 1/3 cup
- Brown sugar, 1/4 cup
- Cloves, 10-12 (whole)
- Bay leaves, 2
- Water

Directions:

1. Preheat your oven to 325°F (165°C).
2. In a large pot, place the corned beef brisket and add enough water to cover the meat. Add bay leaves.
3. Bring to a boil, then reduce the heat and simmer for about 2 hours, or until the meat is tender.
4. Once done, remove the corned beef from the pot and transfer it to a baking dish.
5. In a mixing bowl, combine the whole grain mustard, honey, and brown sugar. Mix until you have a smooth glaze.
6. Brush the glaze generously over the corned beef.
7. Stud the top of the glazed corned beef with whole cloves.
8. Place the corned beef in the oven and bake for an additional 25-30 minutes, or until the glaze is bubbly and slightly caramelized.
9. Remove from the oven, and let it rest for 10 minutes before slicing and serving.

1950s Fact: During the 1950s, various meat glazes and marinades started gaining popularity as households explored new ways to flavor their favorite dishes. Honey-glazed meats, in particular, were a delightful way to blend sweet and savory, and Corned Beef offered a change from the traditional ham or roast.

Cherry Jubilee Flambe

Ingredients:

- Frozen dark sweet cherries, 1 pound (thawed, and juice reserved)
- Granulated sugar, 1/2 cup
- Cornstarch, 1 tablespoon
- Kirsch or brandy, 1/4 cup
- Vanilla ice cream, for serving

Directions:

1. In a saucepan, combine the cherries, their juice, and sugar. Cook over medium heat, stirring occasionally, until the sugar dissolves and the mixture starts to simmer.
2. Mix the cornstarch with 2 tablespoons of water in a small bowl until smooth. Slowly whisk the cornstarch mixture into the simmering cherries.
3. Cook and stir until the mixture thickens and returns to a simmer. Remove from heat.
4. If you're comfortable with flambéing: Heat the kirsch or brandy in a separate small saucepan until warm but not boiling. Pour it over the cherries. Ignite with a long lighter, standing back to avoid the flame. Let the alcohol burn off, leaving the cherries with a wonderful flavor.
5. Serve the cherries warm over scoops of vanilla ice cream.

1950s Fact: Flambe desserts, where alcohol was added and then lit on fire for a dramatic presentation, were a sensation in the 1950s. Cherry Jubilee, in particular, was often served in upscale restaurants, making it a popular choice for special occasions.

Cheese and Vegetable Strata

Ingredients:

- Day-old bread slices, 6
- Butter, 3 tbsp.
- Grated sharp cheddar cheese, 1 1/2 cups
- Frozen mixed vegetables, 1 cup (thawed and drained)
- Eggs, 4
- Milk, 2 cups
- Salt, 1/2 tsp.
- Ground black pepper, 1/4 tsp.
- Dried mustard powder, 1/2 tsp.

Directions:

1. Preheat oven to 350°F (175°C).
2. Lightly butter the bread slices on both sides. Cut them into cubes.
3. In a greased casserole dish, create a layer using half of the bread cubes. Sprinkle half of the cheese and half of the vegetables over the bread. Repeat layers once more with the remaining ingredients.
4. In a mixing bowl, whisk together the eggs, milk, salt, pepper, and mustard powder. Pour this mixture over the layers in the casserole dish.
5. Press the bread down with a fork to ensure it's soaked with the egg mixture.
6. Allow the dish to sit for 10 minutes to let the bread absorb the liquid.
7. Bake in the preheated oven for 45-50 minutes or until set and golden brown on top.
8. Remove from the oven and let it cool for a few minutes before serving.

Swiss Steak

Ingredients:

- Beef round steak, 2 lbs (tenderized)
- All-purpose flour, 1/2 cup
- Salt, 1 tsp
- Black pepper, 1/2 tsp
- Olive oil or vegetable oil, 3 tbsp
- Onion, 1 large (sliced)
- Green bell pepper, 1 (sliced)
- Canned diced tomatoes, 1 can (14.5 oz)
- Worcestershire sauce, 2 tbsp
- Beef broth or water, 1 cup

Directions:

1. In a shallow dish, mix flour, salt, and black pepper. Dredge each piece of steak in the flour mixture, ensuring each piece is well coated.
2. In a large skillet, heat oil over medium-high heat. Once hot, add the steak pieces and brown them on both sides. Remove and set aside.
3. In the same skillet, add the sliced onion and bell pepper. Sauté until they start to soften.
4. Return the steak to the skillet. Pour in the diced tomatoes (with their juice), Worcestershire sauce, and beef broth or water. Make sure the steak is mostly submerged in the liquid.

5. Bring the mixture to a boil, then reduce the heat, cover, and let it simmer for about 1 to 1.5 hours, or until the steak is tender.
6. Serve the Swiss steak hot with mashed potatoes or rice.

1950s Fact: Swiss Steak, despite its name, is not Swiss in origin. The term "swiss" in this context refers to the process of tenderizing meat, making it "swissed." This dish became popular in the 1950s as an economical way to make tough cuts of beef more palatable and tender.

Sloppy Joes

Ingredients:

- Ground beef (1 lb)
- Onion (1, chopped)
- Ketchup (1 cup)
- Mustard (1 tbsp)
- Brown sugar (2 tbsp)
- Hamburger buns

Preparation:

1. In a skillet, brown the ground beef and onion. Drain excess fat.
2. Stir in ketchup, mustard, and brown sugar. Simmer until heated through.
3. Serve the mixture on hamburger buns.

Nutritional Values: Calories: ~300 kcal per serving, Protein: ~15g, Fat: ~10g, Carbohydrates: ~35g

1950s Trivia: Sloppy Joes became a popular fast and easy meal during the 1950s, perfect for feeding a crowd. This messy and flavorful sandwich became a staple at diners, school cafeterias, and family dinners across the country.

Chicken Maryland

Ingredients:

- Chicken pieces (preferably legs and thighs), 4-6 pieces
- Salt and pepper, to taste
- Flour, 1 cup (for dredging)
- Eggs, 2 (beaten)
- Bread crumbs, 1 cup
- Butter, 4 tbsp.
- Cream, 1/2 cup
- White wine or chicken broth, 1/2 cup
- Lemon juice, 2 tbsp.
- Paprika, 1/2 tsp.
- Corn fritters (optional, for serving)

Directions:

1. Preheat the oven to 350°F (175°C).
2. Season the chicken pieces with salt and pepper. Dredge each piece in flour, dip in the beaten egg, and then coat with bread crumbs.
3. In a large skillet, melt the butter over medium heat. Brown the chicken pieces on all sides until they're golden.
4. Transfer the chicken to a baking dish. Pour the wine or chicken broth and cream around the chicken pieces.
5. Sprinkle the chicken with lemon juice and paprika.
6. Cover the baking dish with foil and bake in the preheated oven for 45 minutes or until the chicken is cooked through and tender.
7. Remove the foil for the last 10 minutes of baking to let the chicken become crisp.
8. Serve hot with corn fritters, if desired.

1950s Fact: Though named after the U.S. state of Maryland, Chicken Maryland is also known in other parts of the world, including Australia and the UK. In the 1950s, it was a favored dish for its rich, comforting flavors and the combination of fried chicken with creamy gravy.

Liver and Onions

Ingredients:

- Beef liver (1 lb, sliced)
- Onion (1, sliced)
- Flour (1/2 cup)
- Butter (2 tbsp)
- Salt and pepper to taste

Preparation:

1. Dredge the liver slices in flour seasoned with salt and pepper.
2. In a skillet, melt butter and cook the liver slices until browned on both sides.
3. Add the sliced onions and continue cooking until the onions are soft and caramelized.
4. Serve hot with mashed potatoes or vegetables.

Nutritional Values: Calories: ~300 kcal per serving, Protein: ~25g, Fat: ~15g, Carbohydrates: ~15g

1950s Trivia: Liver and onions was a common meal in the 1950s, often enjoyed for its high nutritional value and affordable ingredients. Despite its divisiveness in taste preference, it remains a memorable dish from this era.

Vegetable Mains

Ratatouille

Ingredients:

- 1 eggplant, diced
- 1 zucchini, diced
- 1 bell pepper, diced
- 1 onion, diced
- 2 tomatoes, diced
- 3 cloves garlic, minced
- 2 tbsp olive oil
- Salt and pepper to taste
- Fresh basil leaves for garnish

Preparation:

1. Heat olive oil in a large skillet over medium heat.
2. Add the eggplant, zucchini, bell pepper, and onion to the skillet and sauté until softened.
3. Stir in the tomatoes and minced garlic, and season with salt and pepper.
4. Cover and simmer for about 20 minutes, stirring occasionally.
5. Garnish with fresh basil leaves before serving.

1950s Trivia: While Ratatouille is a traditional French dish, it gained popularity in the USA in the 1950s as American soldiers returning from World War II brought back a love for European cuisine.

Stuffed Bell Peppers

Ingredients:

- 4 large bell peppers
- 1 cup cooked rice
- 1 can (15 oz) tomato sauce
- 1/2 cup diced onion
- 1/2 cup diced tomatoes
- 1 cup shredded cheese
- Salt and pepper to taste

Preparation:

1. Preheat your oven to 350°F (175°C).
2. Cut the tops off the bell peppers and remove the seeds and membranes.
3. In a bowl, mix together the cooked rice, half of the tomato sauce, onion, diced tomatoes, and half of the shredded cheese. Season with salt and pepper.
4. Stuff the bell peppers with the rice mixture and place them in a baking dish.
5. Pour the remaining tomato sauce over the peppers and top with the remaining shredded cheese.
6. Cover with aluminum foil and bake in the preheated oven for about 30-35 minutes, until the peppers are tender.

1950s Trivia: Stuffed Bell Peppers were a popular and economical dish in the 1950s. They are easy to make and were a perfect way to use leftovers.

Vegetable Casserole

Ingredients:

- 4 cups mixed vegetables (broccoli, cauliflower, carrots), chopped
- 1 can cream of mushroom soup
- 1 cup shredded cheddar cheese
- 1/2 cup breadcrumbs
- 2 tbsp melted butter

Preparation:

1. Preheat your oven to 350°F (175°C).
2. In a large bowl, mix together the chopped vegetables, cream of mushroom soup, and half of the shredded cheddar cheese.
3. Transfer the mixture to a greased baking dish.
4. In a separate bowl, mix the breadcrumbs with melted butter and sprinkle over the vegetable mixture.
5. Top with the remaining cheddar cheese.
6. Bake in the preheated oven for about 25-30 minutes, until bubbly and golden brown.

1950s Trivia: Casseroles became a staple in American households in the 1950s, providing a simple and convenient way to prepare a meal using a single dish. The use of canned soups as a sauce was a hallmark of these recipes.

Green Bean Almondine

Ingredients:

- 1 lb fresh green beans, trimmed
- 1/4 cup slivered almonds
- 2 tbsp butter
- 1 tbsp lemon juice
- Salt and pepper to taste

Preparation:

1. Steam or boil green beans until tender-crisp, about 3-4 minutes.
2. In a skillet, melt butter over medium heat. Add the slivered almonds and sauté until golden brown.
3. Add the cooked green beans to the skillet. Drizzle with lemon juice and season with salt and pepper.
4. Toss everything together, making sure the green beans are well coated with the butter and almonds. Serve warm.

1950s Trivia: In the 1950s, the introduction of frozen vegetables, like green beans, made it easier for home cooks to prepare vegetable dishes without the need for extensive prep work. Green Bean Almondine became popular for its simplicity and elegance.

Glazed Carrots

Ingredients:

- 1 lb carrots, peeled and sliced
- 2 tbsp butter
- 2 tbsp brown sugar
- Salt to taste

Preparation:

1. In a saucepan, boil the carrots until tender. Drain the water.
2. In the same saucepan, melt butter over low heat. Stir in the brown sugar until dissolved.
3. Add the cooked carrots back to the saucepan, and toss them until they are coated with the butter and brown sugar glaze. Season with salt.
4. Cook for an additional 2-3 minutes, allowing the carrots to absorb the glaze. Serve warm.

1950s Trivia: Sweet glazed carrots were a favorite side dish in the 1950s, enjoyed for their natural sweetness enhanced with a simple glaze made from pantry staples.

Creamed Spinach

Ingredients:

- 1 lb fresh spinach
- 1/2 cup heavy cream
- 1/4 cup grated Parmesan cheese
- 1 small onion, finely chopped
- 2 tbsp butter
- Salt, pepper, and nutmeg to taste

Preparation:

1. Wash and chop the spinach. In a large pot, cook the spinach with just the water clinging to the leaves until wilted.
2. In a separate saucepan, melt butter over medium heat. Add the chopped onion and sauté until translucent.
3. Stir in the cooked spinach, heavy cream, and grated Parmesan cheese. Cook until the mixture is heated through.
4. Season with salt, pepper, and a pinch of nutmeg. Serve warm.

1950s Trivia: Creamed Spinach was considered a luxurious side dish in the 1950s, often served in upscale restaurants alongside steak and other meat dishes.

Scalloped Potatoes

Ingredients:

- 4 cups thinly sliced potatoes
- 3 tbsp butter
- 3 tbsp flour
- 2 cups milk
- 1 tsp salt
- 1 small onion, finely chopped
- 1 cup grated cheddar cheese

Preparation:

1. Preheat oven to 350°F (175°C). Butter a baking dish.
2. In a saucepan, melt the butter over medium heat. Stir in the flour and cook for 1-2 minutes.
3. Gradually whisk in the milk, and cook until thickened, stirring constantly. Stir in the salt and onion.
4. Arrange half of the sliced potatoes in the baking dish. Pour half of the sauce over the potatoes.
5. Repeat with the remaining potatoes and sauce. Top with grated cheddar cheese.

6. Cover with aluminum foil and bake for 1 hour, or until the potatoes are tender.

1950s Trivia: Scalloped potatoes were a popular dish in the 1950s, often served as a side dish during family gatherings and holidays. The creamy, cheesy potatoes were comfort food at its finest during this era.

Roasted Butternut Squash

Ingredients:

- 1 large butternut squash
- 2 tbsp olive oil
- 1 tbsp fresh thyme leaves
- 1 tbsp fresh rosemary, chopped
- Salt and pepper to taste

Preparation:

1. Preheat the oven to 400°F (200°C).
2. Peel the butternut squash, cut in half, and remove the seeds. Chop it into 1-inch cubes.
3. Toss the squash with olive oil, fresh thyme leaves, chopped rosemary, salt, and pepper.
4. Spread out on a baking sheet in a single layer.
5. Roast in the preheated oven for about 25-30 minutes or until tender and slightly browned.

1950s Trivia: During the 1950s, roasting vegetables became a popular cooking method. The ease and simplicity of this cooking method allowed the natural flavors of vegetables like butternut squash to shine, making it a favorite dish for family gatherings and holiday meals.

Creamed Peas and Pearl Onions

Ingredients:

- Fresh green peas, 2 cups
- Pearl onions, 1 cup (peeled)
- Butter, 3 tbsp
- All-purpose flour, 2 tbsp
- Whole milk, 1 cup
- Salt and white pepper, to taste
- Nutmeg, a pinch (optional)
- Fresh parsley, for garnish (chopped)

Directions:

1. In a saucepan, boil water with a pinch of salt. Add the peas and pearl onions. Cook until they are tender but not overcooked. This should take about 5 minutes. Drain and set aside.
2. In the same saucepan, melt the butter over medium heat. Sprinkle in the flour, stirring constantly to create a smooth roux. Let it cook for about 2 minutes without letting it brown.
3. Gradually pour in the milk, whisking continuously to avoid any lumps. Bring the mixture to a simmer and let it cook until it thickens, stirring often.
4. Once thickened, add the cooked peas and onions to the saucepan. Gently mix until they are well-coated with the sauce.
5. Season with salt, white pepper, and a pinch of nutmeg if desired.
6. Serve hot, garnished with fresh parsley.

1950s Fact: Creamed dishes were quite popular during the 1950s, as they provided a smooth and rich texture to vegetables, making them more palatable and luxurious. Creamed Peas and Pearl Onions was a classic side dish that paired wonderfully with roasts and other main courses.

Baked Acorn Squash

Ingredients:

- 2 acorn squashes
- 4 tbsp brown sugar
- 4 tbsp butter
- 2 tsp maple syrup
- Salt and pepper to taste

Preparation:

1. Preheat the oven to 400°F (200°C).
2. Cut the acorn squashes in half and scoop out the seeds.
3. Place the squash halves on a baking sheet, cut side up.
4. Place 1 tbsp of butter and 1 tbsp of brown sugar into each half, and drizzle with maple syrup. Season with salt and pepper.
5. Bake in the preheated oven for about 1 hour, or until the squash is tender.

1950s Trivia: Baked acorn squash, often sweetened with ingredients like brown sugar and maple syrup, was a comforting and nutritious dish during the 1950s. As families looked for easy and affordable dishes, acorn squash became a popular choice for a wholesome vegetable main or side dish.

Cabbage Rolls

Ingredients:

- 1 head of cabbage
- 1 cup cooked rice
- 1 onion, finely chopped
- 1 can (14 oz) diced tomatoes

- Salt and pepper to taste

Preparation:

1. Remove the core from the cabbage and blanch the whole head in boiling water just until leaves are pliable.
2. Combine cooked rice, onion, half the tomatoes, salt, and pepper.
3. Place a spoonful of the mixture in the center of a cabbage leaf and roll, tucking in the sides.
4. Place in a baking dish and cover with the remaining tomatoes.
5. Bake at 350°F (175°C) for about 45 minutes.

Fun Fact:

In the 1950s, cabbage rolls were a staple in many American households, often as a means to make use of garden harvests and as an affordable, filling dish during post-war times.

Cauliflower Gratin

Ingredients:

- 1 head of cauliflower, broken into florets
- 2 cups béchamel sauce
- 1 cup grated cheddar cheese
- Salt and pepper to taste

Preparation:

1. Parboil cauliflower florets in salted water for 5 minutes. Drain.
2. In a baking dish, layer the cauliflower, sprinkle with salt, pepper, and half the cheese.
3. Pour over the béchamel sauce and top with the remaining cheese.
4. Bake at 375°F (190°C) for 30 minutes or until golden and bubbly.

Gratins, with their creamy sauce and crispy tops, became a popular side dish in the '50s, often served at family gatherings.

Broccoli and Cheese Casserole

Ingredients:

- 2 cups broccoli florets
- 1 can condensed cream of mushroom soup
- 1 cup grated cheddar cheese
- 1/2 cup milk
- Salt and pepper to taste

Preparation:

1. Steam broccoli until just tender.
2. In a mixing bowl, combine soup, milk, and half the cheese.
3. Add broccoli to a baking dish, pour over the soup mixture, and top with the remaining cheese.
4. Bake at 350°F (175°C) for 25-30 minutes.

Fun Fact:

Casseroles were the ultimate comfort food of the 1950s, and combining veggies with cheese and creamy soup was a hit!

Stuffed Tomatoes

Ingredients:

- 4 large tomatoes
- 1 cup breadcrumbs
- 1/2 cup grated parmesan cheese
- 2 cloves garlic, minced
- Olive oil
- Salt and pepper to taste

Preparation:

1. Slice off the top of each tomato and scoop out the insides.
2. Mix breadcrumbs, parmesan, garlic, salt, and pepper. Drizzle with a bit of olive oil to moisten.
3. Stuff each tomato with the breadcrumb mixture.
4. Bake at 375°F (190°C) for 20 minutes or until tomatoes are tender and tops are golden.

Fun Fact:

Stuffed vegetables became trendy in the 1950s as home cooks looked for ways to incorporate garden produce into hearty mains.

Sweet Potato Casserole with Marshmallows

Ingredients:

- 2 lbs sweet potatoes, peeled and cubed
- 1/4 cup butter
- 1/4 cup milk
- 1/4 cup brown sugar
- 1 tsp vanilla extract
- 2 cups mini marshmallows

Preparation:

1. Boil sweet potatoes until tender. Mash with butter, milk, brown sugar, and vanilla.
2. Transfer to a baking dish and top with marshmallows.
3. Bake at 375°F (190°C) until marshmallows are golden.

Fun Fact:

In the 1950s, the combination of sweet potatoes and marshmallows was seen as the height of culinary creativity, often showcased during Thanksgiving dinners.

Eggplant Parmesan

Ingredients:

- 1 large eggplant, sliced into 1/2-inch rounds
- 2 cups marinara sauce
- 2 cups shredded mozzarella cheese
- 1 cup grated parmesan cheese
- 1 cup breadcrumbs
- 2 eggs, beaten
- Salt and pepper to taste

Preparation:

1. Dip eggplant slices into beaten eggs, then coat with breadcrumbs.
2. Fry in a skillet until golden on both sides.
3. Layer in a baking dish: marinara, eggplant, mozzarella, and parmesan.
4. Repeat layers until all ingredients are used.
5. Bake at 375°F (190°C) for 25-30 minutes.

Fun Fact:

The 1950s saw a surge in Italian-American dishes like Eggplant Parmesan as immigrant influences became mainstream in American homes.

Corn Pudding

Ingredients:

- 4 cups corn kernels (fresh or frozen)
- 4 eggs, beaten
- 2 cups milk
- 2 tbsp sugar
- Salt to taste
- 2 tbsp melted butter

Preparation:

1. Mix all ingredients in a bowl.
2. Pour into a greased baking dish.
3. Bake at 350°F (175°C) for 45-50 minutes.

Fun Fact:

Corn pudding was often a Southern favorite that became popular nationwide in the 1950s, served both as a side and a main dish.

Zucchini Boats

Ingredients:

- 4 large zucchinis
- 1 cup breadcrumbs
- 1/2 cup grated parmesan cheese
- 1/2 cup diced tomatoes
- 1 clove garlic, minced
- Olive oil
- Salt and pepper to taste

Preparation:

1. Slice zucchinis in half lengthwise and scoop out the centers.
2. In a bowl, mix breadcrumbs, parmesan, tomatoes, garlic, salt, and pepper. Drizzle with olive oil.
3. Stuff each zucchini half with the mixture.
4. Bake at 375°F (190°C) for 20-25 minutes.

Fun Fact:

Stuffed vegetables, like zucchini boats, embodied the 1950s' spirit of culinary experimentation while making use of plentiful garden produce.

Creamed Peas and New Potatoes

Ingredients:

- 2 cups fresh peas
- 2 cups new potatoes, peeled and diced
- 2 cups white sauce (béchamel)
- Salt and pepper to taste

Preparation:

1. Boil potatoes until tender. Add peas for the last 5 minutes of cooking.
2. Drain and mix with white sauce. Season with salt and pepper.
3. Serve warm.

Fun Fact:

Creamed dishes, like Creamed Peas and New Potatoes, became a household staple in the '50s due to their simplicity and the creamy comfort they offered.

Spinach Soufflé

Ingredients:

- 2 cups cooked and drained spinach, finely chopped
- 4 eggs, separated
- 2 tbsp butter
- 2 tbsp flour
- 1 cup milk
- 1/2 cup grated gruyere cheese
- Salt and pepper to taste

Preparation:

1. In a saucepan, melt butter and stir in flour. Gradually add milk, stirring until thickened.
2. Remove from heat and mix in spinach, cheese, egg yolks, salt, and pepper.
3. Beat egg whites until stiff peaks form and fold into spinach mixture.
4. Pour into a greased soufflé dish and bake at 375°F (190°C) for 35-40 minutes.

Soufflés were a sign of culinary elegance in the 1950s. They symbolized a sophisticated palate and often featured in more upscale dinner parties.

Brussels Sprouts with Chestnuts

Ingredients:

- 1 lb fresh Brussels sprouts, trimmed
- 1 cup boiled chestnuts, peeled and coarsely chopped
- 3 tbsp butter
- Salt and pepper to taste

Preparation:

1. Boil Brussels sprouts in salted water until just tender.
2. In a skillet, melt butter and sauté chestnuts until slightly browned.
3. Add Brussels sprouts, seasoning with salt and pepper, and toss gently.
4. Serve warm.

Fun Fact:

In the 1950s, Brussels sprouts began to shake their notorious reputation and were embraced in a variety of dishes, particularly during the holiday season.

Mushroom and Barley Casserole

Ingredients:

- 1 cup pearl barley, rinsed
- 3 cups vegetable broth
- 1 lb mushrooms, sliced
- 1 onion, finely chopped
- 3 tbsp butter
- Salt and pepper to taste
- Parsley for garnish

Preparation:

1. Sauté onion and mushrooms in butter until soft.
2. Add barley, vegetable broth, salt, and pepper.
3. Transfer to a casserole dish and bake covered at 350°F (175°C) for about 50 minutes.
4. Garnish with parsley before serving.

Fun Fact:

The 1950s loved casseroles for their convenience and ability to stretch ingredients. Barley, with its hearty texture, became a natural choice for meatless main dishes.

Stuffed Artichokes

Ingredients:

- 4 large artichokes, trimmed
- 1 cup breadcrumbs
- 1/2 cup grated parmesan cheese
- 2 cloves garlic, minced
- Olive oil
- Salt and pepper to taste

- Lemon wedges

Preparation:

1. Prepare a mixture of breadcrumbs, parmesan, garlic, salt, and pepper.
2. Spread open the leaves of the artichokes and stuff with the breadcrumb mixture.
3. Drizzle with olive oil and place in a steaming pot.
4. Steam until the artichokes are tender.
5. Serve with lemon wedges.

Fun Fact:

Artichokes became popular in the 1950s, especially in California. Stuffed artichokes were a sought-after delicacy, often served at garden parties and gatherings.

Turnips in Cream Sauce

Ingredients:

- 4 large turnips, peeled and diced
- 2 cups cream
- 2 tbsp butter
- 2 tbsp flour
- Salt, pepper, and nutmeg to taste
- Parsley for garnish

Preparation:

1. Boil turnips until tender.
2. In a saucepan, melt butter, add flour and stir to create a roux. Slowly add the cream, stirring until thickened.
3. Season with salt, pepper, and a pinch of nutmeg.
4. Add turnips to the sauce, mix well.

5. Garnish with parsley and serve.

Fun Fact:

Turnips, once considered a humble vegetable, saw a renaissance in the
'50s, turning up in creamy, luxurious dishes that showcased its delicate
flavor.

Okra and Tomatoes

Ingredients:

- 1 lb fresh okra, sliced
- 2 cups diced tomatoes
- 1 onion, finely chopped
- 2 cloves garlic, minced
- 2 tbsp vegetable oil
- Salt and pepper to taste

Preparation:

1. Sauté onion and garlic in oil until translucent.
2. Add okra and tomatoes, seasoning with salt and pepper.
3. Simmer until okra is tender.
4. Serve warm as a main or side dish.

Fun Fact:

Okra, primarily popular in the South, began to make its mark
nationwide in the '50s. Paired with tomatoes, it was a summertime
favorite in many American households.

Lentil Loaf

Ingredients:

- 2 cups cooked lentils
- 1 cup breadcrumbs
- 1 onion, finely chopped
- 1 bell pepper, diced
- 2 eggs, beaten
- 2 tbsp tomato paste
- Salt and pepper to taste

Preparation:

1. Mix all ingredients in a large bowl.
2. Press mixture into a greased loaf pan.
3. Bake at 375°F (190°C) for 40-45 minutes or until set.
4. Let cool for a few minutes before slicing.

Fun Fact:

In the '50s, lentil loaf was seen as an economical and nutritious alternative to meatloaf, especially during Lent or for those observing meatless days.

Potato and Onion Gratin

Ingredients:

- 4 large potatoes, thinly sliced
- 2 onions, thinly sliced
- 2 cups heavy cream
- 1 cup grated cheddar cheese
- Salt, pepper, and nutmeg to taste

Preparation:

1. Layer potato and onion slices in a baking dish.
2. Pour over the cream and season with salt, pepper, and a dash of nutmeg.
3. Top with grated cheese.
4. Bake at 350°F (175°C) for 60 minutes or until golden brown and bubbly.

Fun Fact:

Potato dishes were a staple in American households. This gratin version became a trendy side dish at upscale dinner parties in the '50s.

Peas and Carrots in White Sauce

Ingredients:

- 1 cup fresh peas
- 1 cup diced carrots
- 2 tbsp butter
- 2 tbsp flour
- 1 cup milk
- Salt and pepper to taste

Preparation:

1. Cook peas and carrots in boiling water until tender. Drain.
2. In a saucepan, melt butter and stir in flour to form a roux.
3. Gradually add milk, stirring constantly until thickened.
4. Add the peas and carrots to the sauce, season with salt and pepper, and serve.

Fun Fact:

The phrase "peas and carrots" was popularized in the '50s and symbolized items that go well together. The dish itself was a popular accompaniment to mains like roasted chicken.

Collard Greens with Potatoes

Ingredients:

- 1 bunch collard greens, washed and chopped
- 2 potatoes, diced
- 1 onion, chopped
- 2 cloves garlic, minced
- 3 cups vegetable broth
- Salt, pepper, and crushed red pepper to taste

Preparation:

1. In a large pot, sauté onion and garlic until translucent.
2. Add the potatoes and collard greens.
3. Pour in the vegetable broth and season with salt, pepper, and crushed red pepper.
4. Bring to a boil, then simmer until potatoes are tender and greens are wilted.

Fun Fact:

While collard greens have deep roots in Southern American cooking, the '50s saw this leafy vegetable gain popularity across the country, often paired with other staples like potatoes.

Beet and Orange Salad

Ingredients:

- 4 medium beets, cooked and sliced
- 2 oranges, peeled and segmented
- 1/4 cup chopped walnuts
- 2 tbsp olive oil
- 1 tbsp apple cider vinegar
- Salt and pepper to taste

Preparation:

1. Arrange beet slices and orange segments on a plate.
2. Drizzle with olive oil and vinegar.
3. Season with salt and pepper, then sprinkle with chopped walnuts.

Fun Fact:

With the growing popularity of "exotic" fruits like oranges in the '50s, dishes that combined them with traditional vegetables like beets became the talk of the town.

Cocktails

Classic Martini

Ingredients:

- Gin (2 oz)
- Dry vermouth (1 oz)
- Lemon peel or olive for garnish

Preparation:

1. Pour the gin and dry vermouth into a mixing glass filled with ice cubes.
2. Stir well.
3. Strain into a chilled cocktail glass.
4. Garnish with a lemon peel or an olive.

1950s Trivia: In the 1950s, the Martini was the epitome of cool and sophistication. The classic gin and vermouth concoction was enjoyed by many of the decade's biggest stars, like Frank Sinatra and the Rat Pack, making it an iconic drink of the era.

Whiskey Sour

Ingredients:

- Whiskey (2 oz)
- Lemon juice (3/4 oz)
- Sugar (1/2 oz)

- Cherry and lemon slice for garnish

Preparation:

1. Shake the whiskey, lemon juice, and sugar with ice and strain into a whiskey sour glass.
2. Garnish with a cherry and a slice of lemon.

1950s Trivia: The Whiskey Sour was a popular choice in the 1950s, offering a refreshing blend of tart and sweet flavors. It was commonly found at gatherings and cocktail parties, enjoyed by many for its simplicity and timeless taste.

Tom Collins

Ingredients:

- Gin (2 oz)
- Lemon juice (1 oz)
- Simple syrup (1 oz)
- Soda water
- Lemon slice and cherry for garnish

Preparation:

1. Mix the gin, lemon juice, and simple syrup in a Collins glass with ice.
2. Top off with soda water.
3. Garnish with a lemon slice and a cherry.

1950s Trivia: The Tom Collins, named after the old-fashioned Collins glass in which it's served, was another cherished cocktail in the 1950s. It's refreshing, effervescent quality made it a popular choice for summer parties and gatherings.

Pink Lady

Ingredients:

- Gin (1 1/2 oz)
- Applejack (1/2 oz)
- Lemon juice (1/2 oz)
- Grenadine (1/2 oz)
- Egg white (1)
- Cherry for garnish

Preparation:

1. Shake the gin, applejack, lemon juice, grenadine, and egg white with ice.
2. Strain into a cocktail glass.
3. Garnish with a cherry.

1950s Trivia: The Pink Lady cocktail, with its vibrant color and sweet taste, was beloved by many in the 1950s, especially women. The inclusion of egg white gives it a delightful frothy top layer that adds to the drinking experience.

Manhattan

Ingredients:

- Rye whiskey (2 oz)
- Sweet red vermouth (1 oz)
- A few dashes of Angostura bitters
- Maraschino cherry for garnish

Preparation:

1. Pour the ingredients into a mixing glass with ice cubes.
2. Stir well.

3. Strain into a chilled cocktail glass.
4. Garnish with a maraschino cherry.

1950s Trivia: The Manhattan was a classic cocktail that maintained its popularity in the 1950s. It has been enjoyed by many generations for its balanced and robust flavors. It was often seen as an upscale cocktail, enjoyed at elegant dinner parties and events.

Gimlet

Ingredients:

- Gin (2 oz)
- Lime juice (2/3 oz)
- Simple syrup (1/2 oz)

Preparation:

1. Fill a shaker with ice cubes.
2. Add all ingredients.
3. Shake and strain into a cocktail glass.

1950s Trivia: The Gimlet, a classic cocktail from the 1920s, stayed a favorite into the 1950s. It was typically enjoyed as a summer drink, appreciated for its tart and refreshing flavor profile, keeping people cool during the warm months.

Old Fashioned

Ingredients:

- Bourbon or Rye whiskey (2 oz)
- A few dashes Angostura bitters
- 1 sugar cube
- Few dashes plain water

- Orange slice and cherry for garnish

Preparation:

1. Muddle the sugar cube and bitters with one dash of water in a whiskey glass.
2. Fill the glass with ice cubes, add whiskey.
3. Garnish with an orange slice and a cherry.

1950s Trivia: The Old Fashioned is one of the oldest known cocktails, and its timeless appeal carried it through the 1950s as a staple in bars and homes alike. It is simple, yet its flavors are complex and satisfying, appealing to many whiskey lovers.

Mint Julep

Ingredients:

- Mint leaves (about 10)
- Bourbon (2 1/2 oz)
- Sugar (1/2 teaspoon)
- Water

Preparation:

1. Muddle mint leaves and sugar in a collins glass.
2. Fill the glass with crushed ice, add Bourbon.
3. Top with water and stir until the glass becomes frosty.

1950s Trivia: The Mint Julep, often associated with the Kentucky Derby, was a favorite in the South and was enjoyed at various social gatherings in the 1950s. Its refreshing minty taste made it a hit during the warm southern summers.

Daiquiri

Ingredients:

- Light rum (2 oz)
- Fresh lime juice (1 oz)
- Simple syrup (3/4 oz)

Preparation:

1. Pour all the ingredients into a shaker with ice cubes.
2. Shake well.
3. Strain into a chilled cocktail glass.

1950s Trivia: The Daiquiri, associated with Hemingway and the Floridita bar in Havana, continued its popularity in the US throughout the 1950s. It was served as a sophisticated and refreshing beverage at many high-end parties and events.

Harvey Wallbanger

Ingredients:

- Vodka (1 1/2 oz)
- Orange juice (3 oz)
- Galliano (1/2 oz)

Preparation:

1. Pour vodka and orange juice into a highball glass filled with ice cubes.
2. Stir well.

3. Float Galliano on top by pouring it over the back of a spoon so it "floats" on top of the juice.

1950s Trivia: Though its peak was in the 1970s, the Harvey Wallbanger made its appearance in the late '50s. Named after a Manhattan Beach surfer, it's a fun and fruity cocktail that was a hit at many social gatherings.

Sidecar

Ingredients:

- Cognac (2 oz)
- Triple sec (1 oz)
- Lemon juice (3/4 oz)

Preparation:

1. Combine all ingredients into a cocktail shaker filled with ice.
2. Shake until chilled.
3. Strain into a cocktail glass.

1950s Trivia: The Sidecar, a cocktail that predates the 1950s, maintained its position as a cocktail favorite during this decade. It was considered a classy and elegant drink, perfect for ending an evening in style.

Rusty Nail

Ingredients:

- Scotch whisky (1 1/2 oz)
- Drambuie (3/4 oz)
- Lemon twist for garnish

Preparation:

1. Pour the Scotch and Drambuie into an old-fashioned glass filled with ice.
2. Stir well.
3. Garnish with a lemon twist.

1950s Trivia: The Rusty Nail was a popular drink of the 1950s, loved for its smooth, warming flavor with a hint of spice from the Drambuie. It was often enjoyed as an after-dinner drink, perfect for sipping and relaxing.

Brandy Sour

Ingredients:

- Brandy, 2 oz
- Lemon juice, 1 oz
- Simple syrup, 1/2 oz
- Ice cubes
- Lemon slice and maraschino cherry for garnish

Directions:

1. In a shaker, combine brandy, lemon juice, and simple syrup.
2. Add ice cubes to fill the shaker halfway.
3. Shake well until the outside of the shaker is frosty.
4. Strain the mixture into a chilled old-fashioned glass filled with ice.
5. Garnish with a lemon slice and a maraschino cherry.

1950s Fact: While the Whiskey Sour was already a known cocktail before the 1950s, the post-war era saw a rise in variations of the "sour" cocktails. The Brandy Sour became popular in some circles as an alternative for those who preferred the rich flavors of brandy over whiskey.

Tequila Sunrise

Ingredients:

- Tequila (2 oz)
- Orange juice (4 oz)
- Grenadine syrup (3/4 oz)

Preparation:

1. Pour the tequila and orange juice into a highball glass filled with ice cubes.
2. Stir well.
3. Slowly pour the grenadine around the inside edge of the glass. It will sink and gradually rise to mix with the other ingredients.

1950s Trivia: While the Tequila Sunrise gained massive popularity in the '70s, its origins date back to the 1930s and it was enjoyed throughout the 1950s as well. Its beautiful, sunrise-like appearance made it a favorite at gatherings and parties.

Gin Fizz

Ingredients:

- Gin (2 oz)
- Lemon juice (1 oz)
- Sugar (1 teaspoon)
- Soda water

Preparation:

1. Shake gin, lemon juice, and sugar with ice and strain into a highball glass over two ice cubes.
2. Fill with fresh soda water.

1950s Trivia: The Gin Fizz was popular in the 1950s as a refreshing and effervescent cocktail option. It was the drink of choice for many who wanted something light and bubbly with a nice kick from the gin.

Rob Roy

Ingredients:

- Scotch whisky (1 1/2 oz)
- Sweet vermouth (3/4 oz)
- Angostura bitters
- Maraschino cherry for garnish

Preparation:

1. Stir ingredients with ice and strain into a cocktail glass.
2. Garnish with a maraschino cherry.

1950s Trivia: Named after the Scottish hero, the Rob Roy was a beloved cocktail in the 1950s. It's similar to a Manhattan but is made exclusively with Scotch whisky. The drink offered a robust and rich flavor profile that was appreciated by many.

Gin Rickey

Ingredients:

- Gin, 2 oz
- Fresh lime juice, 1 oz
- Club soda, to top up
- Ice cubes
- Lime wheel or wedge, for garnish

Directions:

1. Fill a highball glass with ice cubes.
2. Add the gin and fresh lime juice.
3. Top up with club soda and give it a gentle stir.
4. Garnish with a lime wheel or wedge.

1950s Fact: In the 1950s, the Gin Rickey was seen as a refreshing and lighter alternative to some of the creamier or sweeter cocktails. Its simplicity and the fizz from the club soda made it a popular choice during the hot summer months.

Black Russian

Ingredients:

- Vodka (2 oz)
- Coffee liqueur (1 oz)

Preparation:

1. Pour both ingredients into an old-fashioned glass filled with ice cubes.

2. Stir gently.

1950s Trivia: The Black Russian cocktail was invented in 1949, cementing its place in the 1950s as a popular choice for many. Its simplicity and robust flavor made it a favorite for those who preferred their cocktails straightforward and strong.

Mai Tai

Ingredients:

- Light rum (1 oz)
- Dark rum (1 oz)
- Lime juice (1/2 oz)
- Orange curaçao (1/2 oz)
- Orgeat syrup (1/2 oz)
- Pineapple spear and lime wheel for garnish

Preparation:

1. Shake all ingredients except the dark rum together with ice.
2. Strain into an old-fashioned glass filled with crushed ice.
3. Float the dark rum on top by pouring it over the back of a spoon so it floats.
4. Garnish with a pineapple spear and lime wheel.

1950s Trivia: The Mai Tai, a tropical and exotic cocktail, gained popularity in the 1950s as tiki culture took hold in the United States. The drink is associated with Polynesian-style settings and was often served in tiki bars and restaurants throughout the country.

Desserts

Pineapple Upside-Down Cake

Ingredients:

- Canned pineapple slices
- Maraschino cherries
- Brown sugar (1 cup)
- Cake batter

Preparation:

1. Preheat oven as per the cake batter instructions.
2. In a baking pan, layer brown sugar, pineapple slices, and place a cherry in the middle of each pineapple slice.
3. Pour the cake batter over the arranged pineapples and cherries.
4. Bake according to the cake batter instructions or until a toothpick comes out clean.
5. Once baked, immediately invert the cake onto a serving plate.

1950s Trivia: The Pineapple Upside-Down Cake became a popular household dessert in the 1950s, utilizing the convenient canned pineapple slices. It symbolizes the era's love for sweet, visually appealing, and easy-to-make desserts.

Peach Melba Delight

Ingredients:

- Fresh peaches, 4 (halved and pitted)

- Raspberries, 1 cup
- Granulated sugar, 1/2 cup
- Water, 1 cup
- Lemon juice, 1 tablespoon
- Vanilla ice cream
- Toasted slivered almonds, for garnish (optional)

Directions:

1. In a saucepan, combine the sugar, water, and lemon juice. Bring to a simmer and stir until the sugar has dissolved.
2. Gently place the peach halves in the syrup and poach them until they are tender but still hold their shape, about 5 minutes. Remove the peaches and set them aside to cool.
3. In the same syrup, add the raspberries. Let them cook for about 2-3 minutes. Using a blender or a food processor, puree the mixture until smooth. If desired, you can strain the raspberry sauce to remove the seeds.
4. Chill the raspberry sauce in the refrigerator for at least 1 hour.
5. To serve, place one or two scoops of vanilla ice cream in a dish. Top with a poached peach half (or two). Drizzle with the chilled raspberry sauce and garnish with toasted slivered almonds if desired.

1950s Fact: Peach Melba was a classic dessert, originating in the early 20th century, but it saw resounding popularity in the 1950s, especially at upscale dinners and events. Named after the famous opera singer Nellie Melba, this dish perfectly combines the sweetness of peaches with the tangy flavor of raspberries.

Jell-O Salad II

Ingredients:

- Jell-O or any flavored gelatin

- Mixed fruits or vegetables
- Whipped cream or mayonnaise (optional)

Preparation:

1. Prepare the Jell-O according to the package instructions.
2. Before the Jell-O completely sets, add in the mixed fruits or vegetables.
3. Allow it to set completely and serve with whipped cream or mayonnaise if desired.

1950s Trivia: The Jell-O Salad was a classic 1950s dish, epitomizing the era's fascination with colorful, fun, and innovative food creations. It was a frequent star at potlucks and family gatherings.

Chocolate Fondue

Ingredients:

- Chocolate chips (1 cup)
- Heavy cream (1/2 cup)
- Assorted fruits and marshmallows for dipping

Preparation:

1. Melt the chocolate chips and heavy cream together, stirring until smooth.
2. Transfer to a fondue pot and keep warm.
3. Serve with assorted fruits and marshmallows for dipping.

1950s Trivia: Though more associated with the 1970s, Chocolate Fondue began gaining popularity in the late 1950s as a fun, interactive dessert for parties and gatherings. The dessert was a perfect reflection of the era's love for sociable eating experiences.

Butterscotch Pudding

Ingredients:

- Brown sugar (1 cup)
- Cornstarch (3 tablespoons)
- Salt (a pinch)
- Milk (2 1/2 cups)
- Egg yolks (2, beaten)
- Butter (2 tablespoons)
- Vanilla extract (1 teaspoon)

Preparation:

1. In a saucepan, mix brown sugar, cornstarch, and salt. Stir in milk and cook until thickened.
2. Stir some hot mixture into beaten egg yolks, then blend into the saucepan.
3. Cook for 2 minutes, stirring constantly. Remove from heat, and stir in butter and vanilla.
4. Pour into serving dishes and chill before serving.

1950s Trivia: Butterscotch Pudding was a comforting dessert in the 1950s and was one of the decade's quintessential sweet treats. Its warm, rich flavor was beloved by all, making it a staple in many households.

Cherry Pie

Ingredients:

- Fresh or canned cherries
- Sugar (1 cup)
- Cornstarch (2 tablespoons)
- Pie crust dough
- Butter (2 tablespoons)

Preparation:

1. Preheat oven to 425°F (220°C).
2. Mix cherries, sugar, and cornstarch in a saucepan and cook until thickened.
3. Place one pie crust in a pie dish, pour in the cherry filling.
4. Top with the second crust, creating slits for ventilation, and dot with butter.
5. Bake for about 45-50 minutes or until crust is golden brown.

1950s Trivia: Cherry Pie was a classic and iconic American dessert, especially popular in the 1950s. It was a symbol of warmth and hospitality and frequently featured in diners and family gatherings.

Chocolate Mayonnaise Cake

Ingredients:

- 2 cups all-purpose flour
- 1 cup sugar
- 4 tbsp cocoa powder
- 2 tsp baking soda
- 1 cup mayonnaise

- 1 cup warm water
- 1 tsp vanilla extract

Preparation:

1. Preheat your oven to 350°F (175°C) and grease a cake pan.
2. In a bowl, mix together the flour, sugar, cocoa powder, and baking soda.
3. Stir in the mayonnaise, warm water, and vanilla extract until smooth.
4. Pour the batter into the prepared cake pan and bake for about 30 minutes or until a toothpick inserted comes out clean.

1950s Trivia: The Chocolate Mayonnaise Cake became popular in the 1950s as mayonnaise companies advertised it as a way to make cakes moister. This recipe was a perfect solution during the time when eggs and oil were more scarce.

Ambrosia Salad

Ingredients:

- 1 cup heavy whipping cream
- 1 tbsp sugar
- 1 tsp vanilla extract
- 1 cup pineapple chunks
- 1 cup mandarin oranges
- 1 cup shredded coconut
- 1 cup mini marshmallows
- 1 cup chopped nuts

Preparation:

1. In a bowl, whip together the heavy cream, sugar, and vanilla extract until thick.
2. Gently fold in the pineapple chunks, mandarin oranges, shredded coconut, mini marshmallows, and chopped nuts.

3. Chill the ambrosia salad in the refrigerator for at least 2 hours before serving.

1950s Trivia: Ambrosia Salad became popular in the South in the 1950s. This fruit salad was a festive choice for holiday meals and family gatherings, blending the sweetness of fruit with the richness of cream.

Root Beer Float

Ingredients:

- Root beer
- Vanilla ice cream

Preparation:

1. Place a scoop or two of vanilla ice cream in a tall glass.
2. Pour root beer over the ice cream until the glass is full.
3. Serve with a straw and a long spoon.

1950s Trivia: Root Beer Floats, though invented much earlier, remained a favorite treat in the 1950s, especially at diners and soda fountains, symbolizing the classic American flavors of the era.

Lemon Meringue Pie

Ingredients:

- Pre-made pie crust
- Granulated sugar, 1 1/2 cups
- Cornstarch, 1/4 cup
- Salt, 1/4 teaspoon

- Water, 1 1/2 cups
- Lemons, 2 (juiced and zested)
- Butter, 2 tablespoons
- Egg yolks, 4 (beaten)
- Egg whites, 4
- Cream of tartar, 1/4 teaspoon

Preparation:

1. Pre-bake the pie crust.
2. In a saucepan, combine sugar, cornstarch, salt, water, and lemon juice and zest. Cook until thick and bubbly.
3. Stir a bit of the hot mixture into the beaten egg yolks, then combine with the rest of the hot mixture. Cook for two more minutes.
4. Remove from heat, stir in butter, and pour into the pie crust.
5. Beat egg whites with cream of tartar until soft peaks form. Gradually add sugar and continue beating until stiff peaks form.
6. Spread meringue over the pie filling.
7. Bake at 350°F (175°C) until the meringue is golden brown.

Fun Fact: Lemon Meringue Pie was a refreshing dessert choice in the 1950s, offering a bright and tangy end to a meal.

Strawberry Shortcake

Ingredients:

- Biscuits or shortcakes
- Fresh strawberries, hulled and sliced
- Granulated sugar
- Whipped cream

Preparation:

1. Split the biscuits or shortcakes in half.
2. Spoon strawberries that have been mixed with a bit of sugar over the bottom halves.
3. Top with a dollop of whipped cream and the other half of the biscuit.

Fun Fact: Strawberry shortcake parties became a popular event in the 1950s, signaling the start of summer.

Peach Melba

Ingredients:

- Fresh peaches, 2 (halved and pitted)
- Vanilla ice cream
- Raspberry sauce

Preparation:

1. Blanch the peaches and peel off the skin.
2. Place each peach half in a serving dish and top with a scoop of vanilla ice cream.
3. Drizzle raspberry sauce over the top and serve immediately.

Fun Fact: Though Peach Melba was created much earlier, it saw a resurgence in popularity in the 1950s as a simple yet elegant dessert, often enjoyed at dinner parties and high-end restaurants.

Apple Brown Betty

Ingredients:

- Bread crumbs, 2 cups
- Melted butter, 1/2 cup
- Diced apples, 4 cups
- Sugar, 3/4 cup
- Cinnamon, 1/2 tsp
- Nutmeg, 1/4 tsp
- Lemon zest

Preparation:

1. Mix bread crumbs with melted butter.
2. In a separate bowl, mix apples with sugar, cinnamon, nutmeg, and lemon zest.
3. In a baking dish, alternate layers of the bread crumb mixture and apple mixture.
4. Bake at 350°F (175°C) for 45 minutes or until apples are tender.

Fun Fact: Apple Brown Betty was a popular homey dessert in the 1950s, often made using leftover bread and seasonal apples.

Rice Pudding

Ingredients:

- Cooked rice, 2 cups
- Milk, 2 cups
- Sugar, 1/3 cup
- Salt, 1/4 teaspoon
- Raisins, 1/2 cup
- Vanilla extract, 1 teaspoon

- Ground cinnamon, for garnish

Preparation:

1. Combine cooked rice, milk, sugar, and salt in a saucepan.
2. Cook over medium heat until thick and creamy.
3. Stir in raisins and vanilla extract.
4. Pour into serving dishes and garnish with a sprinkle of cinnamon.

Fun Fact: Rice Pudding was a comfort food favorite in the 1950s, enjoyed as a sweet and creamy treat that was easy and economical to make.

Coconut Cream Pie

Ingredients:

- Pre-baked pie shell
- Coconut milk, 1 cup
- Milk, 1 cup
- Sugar, 3/4 cup
- Cornstarch, 1/4 cup
- Egg yolks, 3
- Shredded coconut, 1 cup
- Whipped cream

Preparation:

1. In a saucepan, combine coconut milk, milk, sugar, and cornstarch. Cook until thickened.
2. Stir some of the hot mixture into the beaten egg yolks, then combine with the remaining hot mixture.
3. Stir in shredded coconut and pour into the pre-baked pie shell.
4. Chill in the refrigerator and top with whipped cream before serving.

Fun Fact: Coconut Cream Pie, with its tropical flavor, was a hit in the 1950s as people sought out diverse and exciting flavors in their desserts.

Devil's Food Cake

Ingredients:

- 1 3/4 cups flour
- 1 1/2 tsp baking powder
- 1 1/2 tsp baking soda
- 3/4 cup cocoa powder
- 2 cups sugar
- 2 eggs
- 1 cup milk
- 1/2 cup vegetable oil
- 2 tsp vanilla extract
- 1 cup boiling water

Preparation:

1. Preheat oven to 350°F (175°C) and grease baking pans.
2. In a bowl, mix flour, baking powder, baking soda, cocoa, and sugar.
3. Add eggs, milk, oil, and vanilla, and mix for 2 minutes.
4. Stir in boiling water until the batter is smooth.
5. Pour into prepared pans and bake for 30-35 minutes.

Fun Fact:

Devil's Food Cake was favored for its rich chocolate taste, contrasting the Angel Food Cake, and became a classic American dessert in the 1950s.

Grasshopper Pie

Ingredients:

- 24 Oreo cookies, crushed
- 1/3 cup melted butter
- 32 marshmallows
- 3/4 cup milk
- 1 1/2 cups heavy cream
- 3 tbsp crème de menthe
- 2 tbsp crème de cacao

Preparation:

1. Mix crushed cookies with melted butter and press into a pie dish.
2. Melt marshmallows with milk, cool the mixture.
3. Whip the cream and fold into the marshmallow mixture.
4. Add crème de menthe and crème de cacao, and pour into the crust.
5. Chill until set.

Fun Fact:

Grasshopper Pie, with its unique mint flavor and vibrant green color, captured the essence of 1950s glamour and fun.

Sponge Cake

Ingredients:

- 6 eggs, separated
- 1 cup sugar
- 1 teaspoon vanilla extract
- 1 cup all-purpose flour
- 1 teaspoon baking powder

- 1/2 teaspoon salt

Preparation:

1. Beat egg whites until stiff.
2. In another bowl, beat egg yolks with sugar and vanilla until creamy.
3. Fold yolk mixture into whites.
4. Sift together flour, baking powder, and salt, and gently fold into the egg mixture.
5. Pour into a tube pan and bake at 350°F (175°C) for 35-40 minutes.

Fun Fact:

Sponge Cake was a light and versatile dessert in the 1950s, often topped with fresh fruits or served with tea.

Blancmange

Ingredients:

- 2 1/2 cups milk
- 1/4 cup sugar
- 2 1/2 tbsp cornstarch
- 1 tsp almond extract
- Chopped almonds for garnish

Preparation:

1. Heat milk in a saucepan until hot but not boiling.
2. Mix sugar and cornstarch and whisk into the milk.
3. Stir constantly until the mixture thickens.
4. Remove from heat and stir in almond extract.
5. Pour into molds and chill until set. Garnish with chopped almonds.

Fun Fact:

Blancmange, a sweet almond-flavored dessert, was an elegant and simple dessert often served at dinner parties in the 1950s.

Custard Pie

Ingredients:

- 2 cups milk
- 4 eggs
- 3/4 cup granulated sugar
- 1 tsp vanilla extract
- 1/4 tsp salt
- 1 unbaked pie crust
- Nutmeg for sprinkling

Preparation:

1. Preheat the oven to 400°F (200°C).
2. Warm milk but do not boil.
3. Beat eggs slightly, and then add sugar, vanilla, and salt.
4. Gradually stir in the milk.
5. Pour the mixture into the unbaked pie crust.
6. Sprinkle with nutmeg.
7. Bake for 25-30 minutes until a knife inserted in the center comes out clean.

Fun Fact:

The Custard Pie was a simple and comforting dessert, beloved for its creamy texture and subtle sweetness during the 1950s.

Date Nut Loaf

Ingredients:

- 1 cup chopped dates
- 1/2 cup chopped nuts
- 1 tsp baking soda
- 1 cup boiling water
- 1 cup sugar
- 1 egg
- 1 3/4 cups flour
- 1/2 tsp salt

Preparation:

1. Combine dates, nuts, and baking soda in a bowl.
2. Pour boiling water over the mixture and let it stand.
3. Beat sugar and egg together and add to the date mixture.
4. Sift in flour and salt, and blend well.
5. Pour into a greased loaf pan and bake at 350°F (175°C) for 45-50 minutes.

Fun Fact:

Date Nut Loaf, packed with dates and nuts, represented the trend of incorporating more fruits and nuts into desserts in the 1950s.

Gingerbread Cookies

Ingredients:

- 2 1/4 cups flour
- 2 tsp ginger
- 1 tsp baking soda
- 3/4 cup butter
- 1 cup sugar

- 1 egg
- 1/4 cup molasses

Preparation:

1. Preheat oven to 350°F (175°C).
2. Sift together flour, ginger, and baking soda.
3. Cream butter and sugar until light and fluffy.
4. Beat in the egg and molasses.
5. Gradually add the sifted dry ingredients.
6. Drop by rounded teaspoons onto ungreased cookie sheets.
7. Bake for 8-10 minutes.

Fun Fact:

Gingerbread cookies, with their warm spices, were a popular homemade treat enjoyed during the holiday season in the 1950s.

Ladyfingers

Ingredients:

- 3 eggs, separated
- 6 tbsp sugar
- 1 tsp vanilla extract
- 1/2 cup flour
- 1/4 tsp baking powder

Preparation:

1. Preheat oven to 350°F (175°C).
2. Beat egg yolks with half the sugar until thick.
3. In another bowl, beat egg whites until stiff, then add the remaining sugar and vanilla.
4. Fold the yolk mixture into the whites.
5. Sift flour and baking powder and gently fold into the egg mixture.

6. Pipe the mixture onto baking sheets in finger shapes.
7. Bake for 8-10 minutes until lightly golden.

Fun Fact:

Ladyfingers were often used in other desserts like trifles and charlottes, showing the versatility of ingredients in the 1950s.

Angel Food Cake

Ingredients:

- 1 1/4 cups egg whites
- 1 1/2 cups sugar
- 1 cup cake flour
- 1 1/4 tsp cream of tartar
- 1 tsp vanilla extract

Preparation:

1. Preheat oven to 375°F (190°C).
2. Beat egg whites until frothy.
3. Add cream of tartar and beat until stiff.
4. Gradually add sugar, continuing to beat.
5. Fold in flour and vanilla gently.
6. Pour into an ungreased tube pan.
7. Bake for 30-35 minutes.

Fun Fact:

Angel Food Cake was often used in the '50s for celebratory events because of its light and fluffy texture, resembling a cloud.

Sour Cream Pound Cake

Ingredients:

- 2 cups sugar
- 1 cup butter
- 6 eggs
- 1 cup sour cream
- 3 cups all-purpose flour
- 1/4 tsp baking soda
- 1 tsp vanilla extract

Preparation:

1. Preheat oven to 325°F (160°C).
2. Cream together sugar and butter.
3. Add eggs one at a time, beating well.
4. Stir in sour cream.
5. Sift together flour and baking soda and add to the mixture.
6. Add vanilla and mix well.
7. Pour into a greased bundt pan.
8. Bake for 1 hour and 20 minutes.

Fun Fact:

Sour Cream Pound Cake was cherished as a rich and moist dessert, perfect for Sunday dinners and gatherings.

French Almond Macarons

Ingredients:

- 1 cup almond flour
- 1 3/4 cups powdered sugar
- 3 egg whites

- 1/4 tsp cream of tartar
- 1/4 cup granulated sugar

Preparation:

1. Preheat oven to 300°F (150°C).
2. Sift almond flour and powdered sugar together.
3. Beat egg whites and cream of tartar until soft peaks form.
4. Gradually add granulated sugar, beating until stiff peaks.
5. Gently fold the dry mixture into egg whites.
6. Pipe small circles onto a lined baking sheet.
7. Let sit for 30 minutes.
8. Bake for 20 minutes.

Fun Fact:

Almond macarons, though of French origin, found a place in American households in the 1950s as a sophisticated and elegant treat for special occasions.

Pecan Pie

Ingredients:

- 1 cup light corn syrup
- 1 cup firmly packed dark brown sugar
- 3 eggs, slightly beaten
- 1/3 cup butter, melted
- 1/2 tsp salt
- 1 tsp vanilla extract
- 1 heaping cup pecan halves
- 1 unbaked deep-dish pie crust

Preparation:

1. Preheat oven to 350°F (175°C).

2. In a large bowl, combine corn syrup, brown sugar, eggs, butter, salt, and vanilla.
3. Mix well.
4. Pour filling into unbaked pie crust; sprinkle with pecan halves.
5. Bake at 350°F for 45 to 50 minutes or until center is set.

Fun Fact:

Pecan Pie, rich and nutty, was a southern classic that swept the nation in the 1950s as a traditional holiday dessert.

Enjoy baking these vintage desserts from the 1950s!

Conclusion

As we close the pages of this 1950s recipe book, we journey back from an era of culinary exploration and nostalgia. The 1950s were a time of post-war optimism, burgeoning technology, and a blossoming of American culture. It was also a time when families sat down at dinner tables, when ingredients were wholesome, and when meals were made from scratch.

These recipes not only offer a taste of dishes popular during the era, but also provide a window into the lifestyles, values, and traditions of mid-20th century America. From simple home-cooked meals to lavish dinner party spreads, the 1950s showcased a blend of comfort and sophistication in its culinary delights.

Whether you're cooking from this book to relive memories, to explore historical flavors, or to introduce classic dishes to a new generation, may the recipes herein bring warmth to your table and joy to your heart. Here's to timeless tastes and the ever-enduring spirit of the 1950s!